Cook. Eat. Drink.
Ramona Valley Wines

*Cookbook and Guide
to Ramona Valley Wines*

SHANNON ROBINSON

Copyright © 2023 by Shannon Robinson

Published by Whimberry Press | https://whimberrypress.com/

First Edition

All rights reserved.

No portion of this book may be reproduced in any form without written permission from the publisher or author, except as permitted by U.S. copyright law.

Neither the publisher nor the author assumes responsibility for any accident, injuries, losses, or other damages resulting from the use of this book.

Want to know more about Ramona, California and its wineries?

Ramona Valley Vineyard Association

https://ramonavalleyvineyards.com/

Ramona Chamber of Commerce

https://ramonachamber.com/

Also, This is **YOUR** book

Write in it, get it messy, change up the recipes, make it ALL yours. Then share your creations on our Social Media channels for everyone to see!

Find, Follow & Share with

@CookEatDrinkRVW

on Facebook & Instagram.

Be sure to tag the winery as well!

Forward

The Ramona Valley Wine Region has grown since its inception in the early 2000s. To experience the growth of a young wine industry is exciting. From zero wineries to its own American Viticultural Area in 2006 to now over 30 wineries and many more vineyards.

To be in the presence of these entrepreneurs who have built an industry from the ashes of a debilitating fire to a burgeoning wine country. They have risked it all to create a new paradigm.

I'm also thankful they have the tenacity to become farmers, learn about the nuances of making wine, and continue studying.

I'm forever grateful to the Ramona Wine Community for embracing me.

Robin Dohrn-Simpson,
Freelance Food, Wine and Travel Writer

Member, The International Food Wine & Travel Writers Association
Business of Wine, SDSU
Marketing and Public Relations Director, Ramona Valley Vineyard Association

www.robindohrnsimpson.com
https://travelwritingbyrobin.blogspot.com

Facebook: robindohrnsimpson
Instagram: robindohrnsimpson
Twitter: @robindohrn

Enjoy!

Welcome to "**Cook. Eat. Drink. Ramona Valley Wines**," a unique cookbook and winery guide that celebrates home cooking paired with Ramona Valley's exceptional wines.

Within these pages, you'll discover a delightful fusion of cherished recipes from friends and family, alongside timeless classics reimagined with a modern twist. This book isn't meant to gather dust on your shelf; it's meant to be your trusty kitchen companion, a well-worn friend filled with notes, highlights, and your personal culinary adventures.

Whether you're whipping up a feast at home or embarking on a wine-tasting journey through the beautiful Ramona Valley, **make this cookbook your own**. Have fun, experiment, and add your unique flavors to these recipes. Cheers to the joy of cooking, eating, drinking, and savoring the flavors of Ramona Valley wines!

Warm regards,

Shannon Robinson
Author, Home Cook & Wine Lover

The Recipes

CHAPTER ONE
Cabernet Sauvignon

Cocktails	8
Appetizers	12
Side Dishes	16
Main Courses	20
Desserts	28

CHAPTER TWO
Chardonnay

Cocktails	34
Appetizers	38
Side Dishes	42
Main Courses	46
Desserts	54

CHAPTER THREE
Merlot

Cocktails	60
Appetizers	64
Side Dishes	68
Main Courses	72
Desserts	80

CHAPTER FOUR
Zinfandel

Cocktails	86
Appetizers	90
Side Dishes	94
Main Courses	98
Desserts	106

CHAPTER FIVE
Sangiovese

Cocktails	112
Appetizers	116
Side Dishes	120
Main Courses	124
Desserts	132

CHAPTER SIX
Syrah

Cocktails	138
Appetizers	142
Side Dishes	146
Main Courses	150
Desserts	158

CHAPTER SEVEN
Viognier

Cocktails	164
Appetizers	168
Side Dishes	172
Main Courses	176
Desserts	184

CHAPTER EIGHT
Tempranillo

Cocktails	190
Appetizers	194
Side Dishes	198
Main Courses	202
Desserts	210

CHAPTER NINE
Malbec

Cocktails	216
Appetizers	220
Side Dishes	224
Main Courses	228
Desserts	236

CHAPTER TEN
Other Varietals

Cocktails	242
Appetizers	246
Side Dishes	250
Main Courses	254
Desserts	262

CABERNET SAUVIGNON
Wine Notes

~ Food Pairing Suggestions ~

Red Meat: Cabernet Sauvignon is a natural partner for red meats like beef, lamb, and venison. Consider classic pairings like a juicy steak or a rich beef stew.

Hard Cheeses: The wine's tannins and acidity complement the bold flavors of hard cheeses such as aged cheddar, gouda, and Parmesan.

Roasted Dishes: Cabernet's structure pairs well with roasted dishes like rosemary-infused roast chicken or a slow-cooked leg of lamb.

Grilled Vegetables: For a vegetarian option, try grilled portobello mushrooms or eggplant, which harmonize with the wine's smoky and earthy notes.

Dark Chocolate: The wine's dark fruit flavors and tannic structure make it an excellent match for dark chocolate desserts.

Herb-Seasoned Dishes: Cabernet Sauvignon complements dishes seasoned with herbs like rosemary, thyme, and mint, enhancing the overall flavor profile.

Burgers and BBQ: Cabernet's robust character stands up to the bold flavors of burgers, barbecue, and grilled sausages.

Game Meats: If you're feeling adventurous, pair Cabernet Sauvignon with game meats like venison or duck.

Tomato-Based Sauces: The wine's acidity complements tomato-based pasta sauces and pizza.

Aged Meat and Stews: Cabernet Sauvignon's complexity shines when paired with dishes like coq au vin or aged beef stew.

PRIMARY FLAVORS
~

Dark Fruits:
Blackcurrant, blackberry, plum.

Herbaceous Notes:
Green bell pepper, mint, eucalyptus (especially in cooler climates).

Spices:
Cedar, tobacco, black pepper.

Oak Influence:
Vanilla, toast, sometimes hints of coconut and baking spices.

TASTE PROFILE
~

Body:
Full-bodied.

Acidity:
Moderate to high, providing structure and freshness.

Tannins:
Firm, often described as grippy or chewy.

Alcohol:
Moderately high.

Finish:
Long and lingering, with a combination of fruit and oak notes.

Chapter One
Cabernet Sauvignon

Welcome to the chapter where wine transcends the glass and finds its way into your kitchen, infusing every dish with a touch of elegance and sophistication. Cabernet Sauvignon, known for its bold and complex character, takes center stage in this culinary adventure.

In the world of wine, Cabernet Sauvignon reigns as a true aristocrat. Its deep, dark fruit flavors, hints of herbs, and sturdy tannins have made it a favorite among connoisseurs. Yet, beyond the wine glass, Cabernet Sauvignon reveals another facet of its personality -- its remarkable prowess as a cooking ingredient.

In these pages, we'll explore the exquisite qualities that make Cabernet Sauvignon the chef's choice. Its robust flavor profile, marked by blackcurrant, plum, and subtle earthy notes, seamlessly marries with a variety of ingredients, elevating dishes to new heights. Whether you're simmering a hearty stew, crafting a rich sauce, or simply looking to enhance the flavors of everyday dishes, Cabernet Sauvignon will become your culinary confidante.

Join us on a journey where the vineyard meets the kitchen, and discover how the regal Cabernet Sauvignon can transform your cooking into an art form. Through these recipes and techniques, you'll learn to harness the magic of this exceptional wine, creating dishes that are nothing short of a gastronomic masterpiece. Prepare to embark on a culinary adventure that celebrates the harmony of food and wine, with Cabernet Sauvignon as your trusted companion.

Cabernet Sauvignon
Berry Vino Smash
COCKTAIL

The Berry Vino Smash combines Cabernet Sauvignon's robust character with the lusciousness of blackberries, creating a berry-packed, wine-infused adventure. Whether with friends or solo, it's a sip of pure berry bliss with a wine country twist. Makes one cocktail, if you're serving a group, simply multiply the ingredients accordingly to make additional servings.

Ingredients:

- 2 oz Cabernet Sauvignon wine
- 1 oz blackberry liqueur (e.g., Crème de Mûre)
- 1/2 oz fresh lemon juice
- 1/2 oz simple syrup (adjust to taste)
- 6-8 fresh blackberries
- Fresh mint leaves, for garnish
- Crushed ice

INSTRUCTIONS:

1. Muddle the Blackberries:
In a cocktail shaker or glass, muddle the fresh blackberries to release their juices and flavors.

2. Add the Cabernet:
Pour in the Cabernet Sauvignon wine.

3. Squeeze in Lemon Juice:
Add freshly squeezed lemon juice for a zesty kick.

4. Sweeten with Simple Syrup:
Sweeten the cocktail with simple syrup to your preferred level of sweetness. Start with 1/2 oz and adjust as needed.

5. Shake or Stir:
If using a shaker, fill it with ice, add the mixture, and shake vigorously for about 10 seconds. If using a glass, stir the ingredients well.

6. Strain and Serve:
Strain the cocktail into a rocks glass filled with crushed ice.

7. Garnish:
Garnish with a sprig of fresh mint and a blackberry on a cocktail pick.

8. Sip and Enjoy:
Savor the Berry Vino Smash, a delightful fusion of Cabernet Sauvignon's depth and blackberries' juicy allure.

NOTES

Cabernet Sauvignon Crush Punch

COCKTAIL

The Cabernet Crush Punch combines Cabernet Sauvignon's rich elegance with brandy's warmth, creating a sophisticated and festive punch. It's a medley of deep red wine, sweet brandy, and fresh fruit, perfect for celebrations or adding flair to your evening. Serves 6-8 glasses.

Ingredients:

- 1 bottle (750 ml) Cabernet Sauvignon wine
- 1 cup brandy
- 1/2 cup orange liqueur (like Triple Sec)
- 1/4 cup freshly squeezed orange juice
- 1/4 cup freshly squeezed lemon juice
- 1/4 cup simple syrup (adjust to taste)
- 1 orange, thinly sliced
- 1 lemon, thinly sliced
- 1 apple, thinly sliced
- 1 cup blackberries
- 1 cup soda water or sparkling water
- Ice cubes

INSTRUCTIONS:

1. Prepare the Fruit:
Thinly slice the orange, lemon, and apple.
Add the fruit slices and blackberries to a large punch bowl.

2. Mix the Punch:
Pour in the Cabernet Sauvignon wine, brandy, orange liqueur, freshly squeezed orange juice, freshly squeezed lemon juice, and simple syrup. Stir to combine.

3. Chill:
Refrigerate the punch for at least 2 hours, allowing the flavors to meld and the fruit to infuse.

4. Add Soda Water:
Just before serving, gently stir in the soda water for a touch of effervescence.

5. Serve:
Fill glasses with ice cubes and ladle the Cabernet Crush Punch over the ice.

6. Garnish:
Garnish each glass with a slice of orange, lemon, and a blackberry or two.

7. Sip and Celebrate:
Enjoy the Cabernet Crush Punch, a burst of wine and brandy magic with a fruity twist.

NOTES

Cabernet Sauvignon
Wine Reduction Crostini

APPETIZER

These Cabernet Sauvignon Wine Reduction Crostinis are the epitome of sophistication and flavor. The rich, velvety wine reduction topping pairs perfectly with crusty baguette slices, creating an appetizer that's both elegant and delicious. Makes approximately 12 crostinis.

Ingredients:

- 1 baguette, thinly sliced
- 1 cup Cabernet Sauvignon wine
- 1/4 cup balsamic vinegar
- 2 tablespoons olive oil
- 2 cloves garlic, minced
- 1 teaspoon fresh rosemary, chopped
- 1/2 teaspoon salt
- 1/4 teaspoon black pepper
- 1/4 cup goat cheese (optional)
- Fresh rosemary sprigs for garnish (optional)

INSTRUCTIONS:

1. Prepare the Baguette Slices:
Preheat your oven to 350°F (175°C). Place the baguette slices on a baking sheet and toast them in the oven for about 5-7 minutes or until they're lightly golden. Remove and set aside.

2. Make the Wine Reduction:
In a small saucepan, combine the Cabernet Sauvignon wine, balsamic vinegar, olive oil, minced garlic, chopped rosemary, salt, and black pepper. Bring the mixture to a simmer over medium heat.

3. Reduce the Wine:
Reduce the heat to low and let the wine mixture simmer gently for about 15-20 minutes, or until it's thickened and reduced by about half. Stir occasionally.

4. Assemble the Crostinis:
Once the wine reduction has thickened, remove it from the heat. Let it cool slightly.

5. Spread the Topping:
Optional: spread a thin layer of goat cheese onto each baguette slice.

6. Add the Wine Reduction:
Spoon a generous amount of the Cabernet Sauvignon wine reduction onto each baguette slice.

7. Garnish:
If desired, garnish each crostini with a small sprig of fresh rosemary.

NOTES

Cabernet Sauvignon
Vino Guacamole

APPETIZER

Cabernet Sauvignon Guacamole is a unique twist on the classic favorite, combining creamy avocados with the rich and robust flavors of Cabernet Sauvignon wine. This appetizer is perfect for wine lovers and guacamole enthusiasts alike. Makes 4-6 servings.

Ingredients:

- 3 ripe avocados, peeled and pitted
- 1/4 cup Cabernet Sauvignon wine
- 1/4 cup red onion, finely chopped
- 1/4 cup fresh cilantro, chopped
- 1 jalapeño pepper, seeded and minced (adjust to your heat preference)
- 2 cloves garlic, minced
- Juice of 2 limes
- Salt and pepper to taste
- Tortilla chips, for serving

INSTRUCTIONS:

1. Prepare the Avocados:
In a mixing bowl, mash the ripe avocados to your desired level of creaminess.

2. Add the Wine:
Pour the Cabernet Sauvignon wine over the mashed avocados and gently fold it in until well combined. The wine will add a rich depth of flavor and a touch of acidity to the guacamole.

3. Incorporate the Ingredients:
Add the chopped red onion, fresh cilantro, minced jalapeño pepper, and minced garlic to the avocado-wine mixture. Squeeze in the juice of two limes. Season with salt and pepper to taste.

4. Mix and Adjust:
Gently stir all the ingredients together until well mixed. Taste and adjust the seasoning, adding more salt, pepper, or lime juice if necessary.

5. Chill and Serve:
Cover the Cabernet Sauvignon Guacamole with plastic wrap, ensuring it touches the surface of the guacamole to prevent browning. Refrigerate for at least 30 minutes to allow the flavors to meld. When ready to serve, transfer the guacamole to a serving bowl and garnish with extra cilantro if desired. Serve with tortilla chips.

NOTES

Cabernet Sauvignon
Roasted Baby Potatoes

SIDE DISH

Cabernet Sauvignon Roasted Baby Potatoes are a flavorful side dish that combines the earthy goodness of baby potatoes with the rich, robust flavors of Cabernet Sauvignon wine. Roasted to crispy perfection and seasoned with herbs and garlic, these potatoes are a delightful addition to any meal. Makes 4 servings.

Ingredients:

- 1 pound baby potatoes, washed and halved
- 1/4 cup Cabernet Sauvignon wine
- 2 tablespoons olive oil
- 4 cloves garlic, minced
- 1 teaspoon dried rosemary (or 1 tablespoon fresh rosemary, chopped)
- 1 teaspoon dried thyme (or 1 tablespoon fresh thyme leaves)
- Salt and black pepper to taste
- Fresh parsley for garnish (optional)

INSTRUCTIONS:

1. Preheat the Oven:
Preheat your oven to 425°F (220°C).

2. Prepare the Potatoes:
Wash the baby potatoes and cut them in half. If they are larger than bite-sized, you can quarter them.

3. Marinate with Wine:
In a large mixing bowl, combine the halved baby potatoes, Cabernet Sauvignon wine, olive oil, minced garlic, dried rosemary, dried thyme, salt, and black pepper. Toss everything together until the potatoes are evenly coated with the wine and seasonings.

4. Roast the Potatoes:
Transfer the potatoes to a baking sheet or roasting pan in a single layer, making sure they are evenly spaced. Roast in the preheated oven for 25-30 minutes, or until the potatoes are golden brown and crispy on the outside, and tender on the inside. You can check for doneness by inserting a fork into a potato; it should go in easily.

5. Garnish and Serve:
Remove the roasted baby potatoes from the oven and garnish with fresh parsley if desired. Serve them hot as a delectable side dish alongside your favorite main course.

NOTES

Cabernet Sauvignon
Baked Macaroni and Cheese

SIDE DISH

Cabernet Sauvignon Baked Macaroni and Cheese is a luxurious twist on a classic comfort dish. This creamy, cheesy mac and cheese is elevated with the deep and rich flavors of Cabernet Sauvignon wine. Makes 6-8 servings.

Ingredients:

- 8 ounces elbow macaroni or pasta of your choice
- 2 cups shredded sharp cheddar cheese
- 1 cup shredded Gruyere cheese
- 1/2 cup grated Parmesan cheese
- 2 cups whole milk
- 1/2 cup Cabernet Sauvignon wine
- 1/4 cup unsalted butter
- 1/4 cup all-purpose flour
- 1/2 teaspoon salt
- 1/2 teaspoon black pepper
- 1/4 teaspoon paprika
- 1/4 teaspoon nutmeg
- 1/4 cup breadcrumbs (for topping)

INSTRUCTIONS:

1. Preheat the Oven:
Preheat your oven to 350°F (175°C) and grease a 9x13-inch baking dish.

2. Cook the Pasta:
Cook the elbow macaroni according to the package instructions until al dente. Drain and set aside.

3. Make the Cheese Sauce:
In a saucepan over medium heat, melt the butter. Stir in the flour to create a roux and cook for about 1-2 minutes until it turns golden brown. Slowly whisk in the milk and Cabernet Sauvignon wine, and cook, stirring constantly until the mixture thickens, about 5-7 minutes.

4. Add Cheese and Seasonings:
Remove the saucepan from the heat and stir in the shredded cheddar, Gruyere, and grated Parmesan cheeses until the sauce is smooth. Season with salt, pepper, paprika, and nutmeg.

5. Combine Pasta and Cheese Sauce:
In a large mixing bowl, combine the cooked macaroni with the cheese sauce, ensuring that the pasta is evenly coated.

6. Transfer to Baking Dish:
Pour the macaroni and cheese mixture into the prepared baking dish, spreading it out evenly.

7. Top with Breadcrumbs:
Sprinkle the breadcrumbs evenly over the top of the macaroni and cheese.

8. Bake:
Bake in the preheated oven for 25-30 minutes, or until the top is golden brown and the cheese sauce is bubbly.

9. Serve:
Remove from the oven and let it cool for a few minutes before serving.

NOTES

~ 19 ~

Cabernet Sauvignon Swedish Meatballs

MAIN COURSE

Cabernet Sauvignon Swedish Meatballs are a rich and savory twist on the classic Swedish meatball recipe. These tender meatballs are simmered in a luscious Cabernet Sauvignon gravy, creating a dish that's bursting with flavor. Makes 4-6 servings.

Ingredients:

For the Meatballs:
- 1 pound ground beef
- 1/2 pound ground pork
- 1/2 cup breadcrumbs
- 1/4 cup milk
- 1 small onion, finely chopped
- 1/2 teaspoon salt
- 1/4 teaspoon black pepper
- 1/4 teaspoon ground allspice
- 1/4 teaspoon ground nutmeg
- 1 egg

For the Gravy:
- 2 tablespoons butter
- 2 tablespoons all-purpose flour
- 1 cup beef broth
- 1/2 cup Cabernet Sauvignon wine
- 1/2 cup heavy cream
- Salt and black pepper to taste

For Serving:
- Cooked egg noodles or mashed potatoes
- Lingonberry sauce (optional)
- Chopped fresh parsley for garnish

INSTRUCTIONS:

1. Prepare the Meatballs:
In a mixing bowl, combine the ground beef, ground pork, breadcrumbs, milk, finely chopped onion, salt, black pepper, ground allspice, ground nutmeg, and egg. Mix until all the ingredients are well combined.

2. Shape the Meatballs:
Shape the meat mixture into 1-inch meatballs. You should get approximately 24 meatballs.

3. Cook the Meatballs:
In a large skillet, heat some oil over medium-high heat. Add the meatballs and cook until they are browned on all sides and cooked through, about 8-10 minutes. Transfer the cooked meatballs to a plate and set them aside.

4. Make the Gravy:
In the same skillet, melt the butter over medium heat. Add the all-purpose flour and cook for 1-2 minutes, stirring constantly, until it turns golden brown.

5. Gradually add the beef broth, Cabernet Sauvignon wine, and heavy cream to the skillet, stirring constantly. Bring the mixture to a simmer and let it cook for about 5-7 minutes, or until the gravy thickens.

6. Combine Meatballs and Gravy:
Return the cooked meatballs to the skillet with the gravy. Simmer for an additional 5-7 minutes, allowing the meatballs to absorb the flavors of the gravy. Season with salt and black pepper to taste.

7. Serve:
Serve over cooked egg noodles or mashed potatoes. Drizzle some of the rich gravy over the meatballs, garnish with chopped fresh parsley, and serve with lingonberry sauce on the side if desired.

NOTES

Cabernet Sauvignon Steak Frites

MAIN COURSE

Cabernet Sauvignon Steak Frites is an elegant yet hearty dish that combines a succulent grilled steak with crispy golden french fries. The steak is bathed in a luscious Cabernet Sauvignon reduction, making every bite a flavorful experience. Makes 2-4 servings.

Ingredients:

For the Steak:
- 2 boneless ribeye or sirloin steaks (8-10 ounces each)
- Salt and black pepper to taste
- 2 tablespoons olive oil
- 2 cloves garlic, minced
- 2 sprigs fresh rosemary

For the Fries:
- 4 large russet potatoes, peeled and cut into matchstick-sized fries
- Vegetable oil for frying
- Salt to taste

For the Cabernet Sauvignon Reduction:
- 1 cup Cabernet Sauvignon wine
- 1/4 cup beef broth
- 2 tablespoons unsalted butter
- 1 shallot, finely chopped
- Salt and black pepper to taste

INSTRUCTIONS:

NOTES

1. Prepare the Steak:
Season the steaks generously with salt and black pepper on both sides. In a skillet or on a grill, heat the olive oil over high heat. Add the minced garlic and fresh rosemary sprigs. Sear the steaks for about 3-4 minutes per side for medium-rare, or adjust the cooking time to your desired level of doneness. Remove the steaks from the heat, tent them with foil, and let them rest while preparing the reduction.

2. Make the Cabernet Sauvignon Reduction:
In a saucepan, melt the butter over medium heat. Add the finely chopped shallot and sauté until it becomes translucent. Pour in the Cabernet Sauvignon wine and beef broth. Bring the mixture to a boil, then reduce the heat and simmer for about 15-20 minutes, or until it reduces by half and thickens. Season with salt and black pepper to taste.

3. Prepare the Fries:
While the reduction is simmering, heat vegetable oil in a deep fryer or large pot to 350°F (175°C). Carefully add the matchstick-sized potato fries and fry until they are golden brown and crispy, about 4-6 minutes. Remove the fries with a slotted spoon and place them on paper towels to drain. Sprinkle with salt immediately.

4. Serve:
Place the rested steaks on serving plates. Drizzle the Cabernet Sauvignon reduction over each steak. Serve with a generous portion of crispy golden fries on the side.

Cabernet Sauvignon Meatloaf

MAIN COURSE

Cabernet Sauvignon Meatloaf is a rich and savory twist on the classic comfort food. This hearty meatloaf is generously seasoned, and its flavorful depth is enhanced by the addition of Cabernet Sauvignon wine, making it a satisfying family favorite. Makes 6-8 servings.

Ingredients:

For the Meatloaf:
- 2 pounds ground beef (85% lean)
- 1 cup breadcrumbs
- 1/2 cup Cabernet Sauvignon wine
- 1 onion, finely chopped
- 2 cloves garlic, minced
- 2 large eggs
- 1/4 cup milk
- 1/4 cup ketchup
- 2 tablespoons Worcestershire sauce
- 1 tablespoon Dijon mustard
- 1 teaspoon salt
- 1/2 teaspoon black pepper
- 1/2 teaspoon dried thyme
- 1/2 teaspoon dried rosemary
- 1/4 teaspoon dried oregano

For the Glaze:
- 1/2 cup ketchup
- 2 tablespoons brown sugar
- 2 tablespoons Cabernet Sauvignon wine

Instructions:

1. Preheat the Oven:
Preheat your oven to 350°F (175°C).

2. Prepare the Meatloaf Mixture:
In a large mixing bowl, combine the ground beef, breadcrumbs, Cabernet Sauvignon wine, chopped onion, minced garlic, eggs, milk, 1/4 cup ketchup, Worcestershire sauce, Dijon mustard, salt, black pepper, dried thyme, dried rosemary, and dried oregano. Mix until all the ingredients are well combined.

3. Shape the Meatloaf:
Shape the mixture into a loaf shape and place it in a baking dish or on a lined baking sheet.

4. Make the Glaze:
In a small bowl, mix together 1/2 cup ketchup, brown sugar, and 2 tablespoons of Cabernet Sauvignon wine.

5. Glaze and Bake:
Brush the glaze over the top of the meatloaf, covering it evenly. Bake in the preheated oven for about 1 hour or until the internal temperature reaches 160°F (70°C) and the meatloaf is cooked through.

6. Rest and Serve:
Remove the meatloaf from the oven and let it rest for 10 minutes before slicing. This allows the juices to redistribute, keeping the meatloaf moist.

7. Serve:
Slice into thick slices and serve it alongside your favorite sides, such as mashed potatoes and green beans.

Notes

Cabernet Sauvignon Beef Stroganoff

MAIN COURSE

Cabernet Sauvignon Beef Stroganoff is a luxurious and hearty dish that combines tender strips of beef with a rich and velvety Cabernet Sauvignon-infused mushroom sauce. This classic comfort food is elevated with the depth and complexity of red wine. Makes 4-6 servings.

Ingredients:

- 1 pound beef sirloin or tenderloin, thinly sliced into strips
- 2 tablespoons olive oil
- 1 onion, finely chopped
- 2 cloves garlic, minced
- 8 ounces mushrooms, sliced
- 1/4 cup Cabernet Sauvignon wine
- 1 cup beef broth
- 2 tablespoons all-purpose flour
- 1 cup sour cream
- 1 teaspoon Dijon mustard
- 1 teaspoon Worcestershire sauce
- Salt and black pepper to taste
- Fresh parsley, chopped, for garnish
- 12 ounces egg noodles or your choice of pasta, cooked and drained

Instructions:

Notes

1. Cook the Beef:
In a large skillet, heat the olive oil over medium-high heat. Add the thinly sliced beef and cook until browned on all sides, about 2-3 minutes. Remove the beef from the skillet and set it aside.

2. Saute the Onion, Garlic, and Mushrooms:
In the same skillet, add the chopped onion and minced garlic. Saute for 2-3 minutes until the onion becomes translucent. Add the sliced mushrooms and cook until they release their moisture and start to brown, about 5-7 minutes.

3. Make the Wine Sauce:
Sprinkle the flour over the mushroom mixture and stir well to combine. Pour in the Cabernet Sauvignon wine and beef broth, stirring constantly. Bring the mixture to a simmer and cook for 5 minutes until it thickens.

4. Add the Beef Back In:
Return the cooked beef to the skillet and stir to coat it with the sauce. Simmer for an additional 5 minutes to heat the beef through.

5. Finish the Sauce:
Stir in the sour cream, Dijon mustard, and Worcestershire sauce. Season with salt and black pepper to taste. Cook for an additional 2 minutes until the sauce is heated through and creamy.

6. Serve:
Serve over cooked and drained egg noodles or your choice of pasta. Garnish with chopped fresh parsley.

Cabernet Sauvignon Strawberry Shortcake

DESSERT

Cabernet Sauvignon Strawberry Shortcake is a delightful twist on the classic dessert. This recipe pairs juicy strawberries macerated in Cabernet Sauvignon wine with homemade shortcakes and whipped cream for a delectable treat. Makes 6 servings.

Ingredients:

For the Strawberry Filling:
- 1 pound fresh strawberries, hulled and sliced
- 1/2 cup Cabernet Sauvignon wine
- 1/4 cup granulated sugar
- 1 teaspoon lemon juice
- Zest of 1 lemon

For the Shortcakes:
- 2 cups all-purpose flour
- 1/4 cup granulated sugar
- 1 tablespoon baking powder
- 1/2 teaspoon salt
- 1/2 cup (1 stick) cold unsalted butter, cubed
- 2/3 cup whole milk
- 1 teaspoon vanilla extract

For the Whipped Cream:
- 1 cup heavy cream
- 2 tablespoons powdered sugar
- 1 teaspoon vanilla extract

INSTRUCTIONS:

NOTES

1. Prepare the Strawberry Filling:
In a mixing bowl, combine the sliced strawberries, Cabernet Sauvignon wine, granulated sugar, lemon juice, and lemon zest. Toss to coat the strawberries evenly. Cover and refrigerate for at least 30 minutes to allow the flavors to meld.

2. Make the Shortcakes:
Preheat your oven to 425°F (220°C). In a large mixing bowl, whisk together the flour, granulated sugar, baking powder, and salt. Add the cold, cubed butter and use a pastry cutter or your fingers to work the butter into the dry ingredients until the mixture resembles coarse crumbs.

3. **Pour in** the milk and vanilla extract. Stir until the dough just comes together.

4. **Turn the dough out** onto a floured surface and gently knead it a few times until it forms a cohesive ball. Pat the dough to about 1-inch thickness.

5. **Use a round biscuit cutter** (about 3 inches in diameter) to cut out shortcakes. Place them on a baking sheet lined with parchment paper.

6. **Bake in the preheated oven** for 12-15 minutes or until the shortcakes are golden brown. Remove from the oven and let them cool slightly.

7. Prepare the Whipped Cream:
In a chilled mixing bowl, beat the heavy cream, powdered sugar, and vanilla extract until stiff peaks form.

8. Assemble the Shortcakes:
Slice the baked shortcakes in half horizontally. Spoon a generous portion of the Cabernet Sauvignon macerated strawberries onto the bottom half. Top with a dollop of whipped cream and then the other half of the shortcake. Repeat for each serving.

9. Serve:
Serve immediately. Optionally, garnish with a fresh strawberry or a sprig of mint for an extra touch of elegance.

Cabernet Sauvignon Chocolate Pound Cake

DESSERT

Cabernet Sauvignon Chocolate Pound Cake is a decadent dessert that combines the rich flavors of dark chocolate with the depth of Cabernet Sauvignon wine. This cake is moist, tender, and perfect for chocolate lovers with a hint of wine sophistication. Makes 10-12 servings.

Ingredients:

For the Chocolate Pound Cake:
- 1 3/4 cups all-purpose flour
- 3/4 cup unsweetened cocoa powder
- 2 teaspoons baking powder
- 1/2 teaspoon baking soda
- 1/2 teaspoon salt
- 1 cup unsalted butter, softened
- 1 1/2 cups granulated sugar
- 4 large eggs
- 1 teaspoon vanilla extract
- 1 cup Cabernet Sauvignon wine

For the Chocolate Ganache:
- 6 ounces dark chocolate, finely chopped
- 1/2 cup heavy cream

Instructions:

1. Preheat and Prepare:
Preheat your oven to 325°F (163°C). Grease and flour a 10-inch (12-cup) bundt pan or a pound cake pan.

2. Mix Dry Ingredients:
In a medium-sized bowl, whisk together the all-purpose flour, cocoa powder, baking powder, baking soda, and salt. Set this dry mixture aside.

3. Cream Butter and Sugar:
In a large mixing bowl, using an electric mixer, cream together the softened butter and granulated sugar until light and fluffy, about 3-4 minutes.

4. Add Eggs and Vanilla:
Beat in the eggs, one at a time, ensuring each egg is fully incorporated before adding the next one. Stir in the vanilla extract.

5. Alternate Dry and Wine:
Gradually add the dry mixture to the butter and sugar mixture, alternating with the Cabernet Sauvignon wine, beginning and ending with the dry mixture. Mix until just combined.

Notes

6. Bake:
Pour the cake batter into the prepared bundt or pound cake pan. Smooth the top with a spatula. Bake in the preheated oven for 50-60 minutes or until a toothpick inserted into the center comes out clean or with a few moist crumbs attached.

7. Cool:
Allow the cake to cool in the pan for about 10 minutes, then invert it onto a wire rack to cool completely.

8. Make the Chocolate Ganache:
Place the finely chopped dark chocolate in a heatproof bowl. In a saucepan, heat the heavy cream until it simmers (do not boil). Pour the hot cream over the chopped chocolate and let it sit for 1-2 minutes. Stir until the chocolate is completely melted and the mixture is smooth.

9. Glaze the Cake:
Pour the chocolate ganache over the cooled pound cake, allowing it to drizzle down the sides. Let the ganache set for about 15-20 minutes. Slice and serve.

Chardonnay
Wine Notes

~ Food Pairing Suggestions ~

Seafood: Chardonnay's bright acidity pairs wonderfully with seafood. Try it with grilled shrimp, lobster, or seared scallops.

Poultry: Chardonnay complements chicken dishes, whether roasted, grilled, or in creamy sauces.

Creamy Pasta Dishes: Its buttery and full-bodied style harmonizes with creamy pasta sauces like Alfredo or carbonara.

Mild Cheeses: Chardonnay pairs well with soft and semi-soft cheeses such as brie, camembert, and young gouda.

Salads: For lighter Chardonnays, pair with salads featuring vinaigrette dressings, goat cheese, and fruits like apples or pears.

White Meats: It's a versatile choice for pork tenderloin, turkey, and veal dishes.

Vegetarian Dishes: Chardonnay can complement vegetarian dishes like risotto with mushrooms or butternut squash.

Shellfish: Its crispness is ideal for shellfish like oysters, clams, and mussels.

Herb-Seasoned Dishes: Chardonnay pairs well with dishes seasoned with fresh herbs, enhancing the wine's citrus and mineral notes.

Buttery Popcorn: For a fun pairing, try a buttery Chardonnay with your favorite popcorn for a movie night treat.

PRIMARY FLAVORS
~

Fruit Notes:
Apple, pear, citrus (lemon, lime), sometimes tropical fruits like pineapple and mango.

Oak Influence:
Vanilla, butter, caramel, baking spices (when oak-aged).

Mineral Notes:
Particularly in wines from cooler climates, you might detect hints of flint or chalk.

TASTE PROFILE
~

Body:
Varies from light to full-bodied, depending on the winemaking style.

Acidity:
Moderate to high, providing freshness and balance.

Oak and Butter:
Presence varies widely; some Chardonnays are unoaked or lightly oaked, while others are rich and buttery due to oak aging and malolactic fermentation.

Alcohol:
Moderate.

Finish:
Can range from crisp and clean to creamy and lingering, depending on winemaking choices.

Chapter Two
Chardonnay

Step into a world where culinary delight meets the elegance of Chardonnay wine. Welcome to a chapter that explores the multifaceted qualities of Chardonnay, not just as a wine for sipping, but as a secret ingredient that elevates your dishes to the extraordinary.

Chardonnay, often praised as the "queen of white wines," has enchanted wine enthusiasts for generations with its remarkable diversity. In this culinary journey, we'll peel back the layers of this beloved varietal, unlocking its secrets for the kitchen.

Chardonnay is revered for its versatility, and its flavor profile, marked by notes of green apple, citrus, and hints of oak, offers a canvas for culinary creativity. Its vibrant acidity and ability to harmonize with a spectrum of ingredients make it a formidable ally in the kitchen. From delicate seafood to creamy pastas, from roasted chicken to decadent desserts, Chardonnay has a place in every corner of the culinary world.

As we delve into this chapter, you'll discover how to infuse your dishes with the elegance and sophistication of Chardonnay. Whether you're a seasoned chef or an enthusiastic home cook, these recipes and techniques will empower you to master the art of cooking with Chardonnay, unlocking flavors that dance on your taste buds. Let us embark on a gastronomic journey where the world of Chardonnay unfolds not just in your glass but on your plate as well.

Chardonnay Sunshine Sipper
COCKTAIL

The Chardonnay Sunshine Sipper combines Chardonnay's buttery notes with citrus for a smooth, refreshing elixir. Whether on the patio or celebrating, it's your passport to a sip of sunshine. Makes one serving, multiply for more!

Ingredients:

- 2 oz Chardonnay wine
- 1 oz orange liqueur (like Triple Sec or Cointreau)
- 1/2 oz freshly squeezed lemon juice
- 1/2 oz freshly squeezed lime juice
- 1/2 oz simple syrup (adjust to taste)
- Ice cubes
- Lemon and lime slices, for garnish
- Fresh mint leaves, for garnish

INSTRUCTIONS:

1. Prepare Your Glass:
Fill a glass with ice cubes to chill it while you prepare the cocktail.

2. Shake the Ingredients:
In a cocktail shaker, combine the Chardonnay wine, orange liqueur, freshly squeezed lemon juice, freshly squeezed lime juice, and simple syrup.

3. Shake Vigorously:
Shake the mixture vigorously for about 10-15 seconds to chill and combine the ingredients.

4. Strain and Serve:
Discard the ice from the prepared glass.
Strain the cocktail mixture into the chilled glass.

5. Garnish:
Garnish with a slice of lemon and a slice of lime. Add a sprig of fresh mint for an extra burst of aroma and flavor.

6. Serve and Enjoy:
Raise your Chardonnay Citrus Sipper, toast to the moment, and enjoy the refreshing blend of Chardonnay and citrus.

NOTES

Chardonnay Cabana Cooler

COCKTAIL

The Chardonnay Cabana Cooler is a tropical escape, blending Chardonnay's sophistication with rum's island vibes. Sip on this refreshing elixir and let it transport you to a beachside cabana in an instant. Makes one serving, multiply for more!

Ingredients:

- 2 oz Chardonnay wine
- 1 oz white rum
- 1 oz coconut cream
- 1 oz pineapple juice
- 1/2 oz freshly squeezed lime juice
- 1/2 oz simple syrup (adjust to taste)
- Ice cubes
- Pineapple slice and maraschino cherry, for garnish
- Fresh mint sprig, for garnish

Instructions:

1. Prepare Your Glass:
Fill a highball or tiki glass with ice cubes to chill it while you prepare the cocktail.

2. Shake the Ingredients:
In a cocktail shaker, combine the Chardonnay wine, white rum, coconut cream, pineapple juice, freshly squeezed lime juice, and simple syrup.

3. Shake Vigorously:
Shake the mixture vigorously for about 10-15 seconds to chill and combine the ingredients.

4. Strain and Serve:
Discard the ice from the prepared glass. Strain the cocktail mixture into the chilled glass over fresh ice.

5. Garnish:
Garnish your Chardonnay Cabana Cooler with a slice of pineapple and a maraschino cherry. Add a sprig of fresh mint for an extra tropical touch.

Notes

Chardonnay
Creamy Spinach Artichoke Dip

APPETIZER

Creamy Chardonnay Spinach Artichoke Dip is a luscious appetizer that combines the richness of Chardonnay wine with the classic flavors of spinach and artichoke. This warm and cheesy dip is the ultimate crowd-pleaser, perfect for sharing at gatherings or enjoying as a cozy snack. Makes 6-8 servings.

Ingredients:

- 1 (10-ounce) package of frozen chopped spinach, thawed and drained
- 1 (14-ounce) can of artichoke hearts, drained and chopped
- 1 cup grated Parmesan cheese
- 1 cup shredded mozzarella cheese
- 1 cup mayonnaise
- 1/2 cup sour cream
- 1/2 cup Chardonnay wine
- 1/4 cup diced onions
- 2 cloves garlic, minced
- 1/2 teaspoon salt
- 1/2 teaspoon black pepper
- 1/4 teaspoon crushed red pepper flakes (optional, for heat)
- Tortilla chips, crackers, or bread slices for serving

Instructions:

1. Preheat the Oven:
Preheat your oven to 375°F (190°C).

2. Combine Ingredients:
In a large mixing bowl, combine the chopped spinach, chopped artichoke hearts, grated Parmesan cheese, shredded mozzarella cheese, mayonnaise, sour cream, Chardonnay wine, diced onions, minced garlic, salt, black pepper, and crushed red pepper flakes (if using). Stir until all the ingredients are well combined.

3. Transfer to Baking Dish:
Spoon the mixture into a baking dish (approximately 8x8 inches or equivalent). Spread it evenly.

4. Bake:
Place the baking dish in the preheated oven and bake for about 25-30 minutes, or until the dip is hot, bubbly, and lightly golden on top.

5. Serve:
Remove the dip from the oven and let it cool slightly. Serve with tortilla chips, crackers, or slices of toasted bread.

Notes

Chardonnay Buffalo Chicken Dip

APPETIZER

Chardonnay Buffalo Chicken Dip is a creamy and tangy appetizer that combines the zesty flavors of buffalo chicken with the richness of Chardonnay wine. It's a crowd-pleasing dip that adds a touch of sophistication to your game day or party spread. Makes 6-8 servings.

Ingredients:

- 2 cups cooked chicken breast, shredded
- 1/2 cup Chardonnay wine
- 1/2 cup hot sauce (adjust to your preferred level of spiciness)
- 8 oz cream cheese, softened
- 1/2 cup sour cream
- 1/2 cup mayonnaise
- 1 cup shredded cheddar cheese
- 1/2 cup crumbled blue cheese (optional, for extra flavor)
- 1 teaspoon garlic powder
- 1 teaspoon onion powder
- 1/2 teaspoon black pepper
- 1/2 teaspoon salt
- Celery sticks, carrot sticks, or tortilla chips for serving

Instructions:

1. Preheat the Oven:
Preheat your oven to 350°F (175°C).

2. Prepare the Chicken:
In a large skillet over medium heat, cook the chicken until fully cooked and no longer pink. Shred the cooked chicken using two forks.

3. Combine Ingredients:
In a mixing bowl, combine the shredded chicken, Chardonnay wine, hot sauce, softened cream cheese, sour cream, mayonnaise, shredded cheddar cheese, crumbled blue cheese (if using), garlic powder, onion powder, black pepper, and salt. Mix until all the ingredients are well combined.

4. Transfer to Baking Dish:
Spoon the mixture into a baking dish (approximately 8x8 inches or equivalent). Spread it evenly.

5. Bake:
Place the baking dish in the preheated oven and bake for about 25-30 minutes, or until the dip is hot, bubbly, and lightly golden on top.

6. Serve:
Remove from the oven and let it cool slightly. Serve it with celery sticks, carrot sticks, or tortilla chips.

Notes

Chardonnay Glazed Carrot Medley

SIDE DISH

The Chardonnay-Glazed Carrot Medley is a delightful dish that combines the earthy sweetness of carrots with the subtle elegance of Chardonnay wine. These tender, glazed carrots are a perfect harmony of flavors and make for a dish that's both comforting and sophisticated. Makes 4-6 servings.

Ingredients:

- 1 lb (450g) baby carrots, or peeled and sliced into bite-sized pieces
- 1/2 cup Chardonnay wine
- 2 tablespoons unsalted butter
- 2 tablespoons honey
- 1 teaspoon fresh thyme leaves
- Salt and black pepper to taste
- Fresh parsley for garnish (optional)

INSTRUCTIONS:

1. Cook the Carrots:
In a large skillet, melt the butter over medium heat. Add the baby carrots and cook for about 5 minutes, stirring occasionally, until they start to become tender.

2. Add the Chardonnay Wine:
Pour in the Chardonnay wine and honey. Stir to combine.

3. Simmer and Glaze:
Reduce the heat to low, cover the skillet, and let the carrots simmer in the wine and honey mixture for about 15-20 minutes, or until they are fork-tender and the liquid has reduced into a glossy glaze.

4. Season and Garnish:
Sprinkle fresh thyme leaves over the glazed carrots and season with salt and black pepper to taste. If desired, garnish with fresh parsley for a pop of color.

5. Serve:
Transfer to a serving platter. This dish can be served warm or at room temperature.

NOTES

Chardonnay Waldorf Salad

SIDE DISH

Chardonnay Waldorf Salad is a refreshing twist on the classic Waldorf salad, combining crisp apples, crunchy celery, sweet grapes, and toasted walnuts in a creamy Chardonnay-infused dressing. It's a delightful side dish or light meal with a touch of wine-inspired sophistication. Makes 4-6 servings.

Ingredients:

For the Salad:
- 3 large apples, cored and diced (use a mix of red and green apples for variety)
- 2 cups seedless red grapes, halved
- 2 cups celery, thinly sliced
- 1 cup toasted walnuts, coarsely chopped
- 1/4 cup fresh parsley leaves, chopped (for garnish, optional)

For the Chardonnay Dressing:
- 1/2 cup mayonnaise
- 1/2 cup plain Greek yogurt
- 1/4 cup Chardonnay wine
- 2 tablespoons honey
- 1 tablespoon lemon juice
- Salt and black pepper to taste

INSTRUCTIONS:

1. Prepare the Chardonnay Dressing:
In a small mixing bowl, whisk together the mayonnaise, Greek yogurt, Chardonnay wine, honey, lemon juice, salt, and black pepper until the dressing is well combined. Adjust the sweetness and seasoning to your taste. Refrigerate the dressing while preparing the salad.

2. Toast the Walnuts:
Preheat your oven to 350°F (175°C). Place the walnuts on a baking sheet and toast them for about 5-7 minutes or until they become fragrant and lightly golden. Remove from the oven and let them cool before chopping.

3. Combine Salad Ingredients:
In a large salad bowl, combine the diced apples, halved grapes, sliced celery, and toasted walnuts. Toss them gently to distribute the ingredients evenly.

4. Add the Dressing:
Pour the chilled Chardonnay dressing over the salad. Gently toss until all the ingredients are well coated with the dressing.

5. Chill:
Cover the salad bowl with plastic wrap and refrigerate for at least 30 minutes before serving to allow the flavors to meld.

6. Serve:
When ready to serve, garnish with fresh parsley leaves, if desired. Serve as a delightful side dish or a light and refreshing meal.

NOTES

Chardonnay Chicken and Dumplings

MAIN COURSE

Chardonnay Chicken and Dumplings is a luxurious twist on a classic comfort food. Tender chicken, hearty vegetables, and fluffy dumplings are simmered in a creamy Chardonnay-infused broth, creating a dish that's both comforting and elegant. Makes 4-6 servings.

Ingredients:

For the Chicken and Broth:
- 2 lbs boneless, skinless chicken thighs
- 2 tablespoons olive oil
- 1 onion, finely chopped
- 3 carrots, sliced
- 3 celery stalks, sliced
- 3 cloves garlic, minced
- 1 cup Chardonnay wine
- 6 cups chicken broth
- 2 bay leaves
- Salt and black pepper to taste

For the Dumplings:
- 2 cups all-purpose flour
- 1 tablespoon baking powder
- 1/2 teaspoon salt
- 1/4 cup unsalted butter, cold and cubed
- 3/4 cup milk
- 2 tablespoons fresh parsley, chopped (for garnish, optional)

Instructions:

1. Sear the Chicken:
In a large pot or Dutch oven, heat the olive oil over medium-high heat. Season the chicken thighs with salt and black pepper, then sear them in the hot oil until golden brown on both sides. Remove the chicken and set it aside.

2. Sauté the Vegetables:
In the same pot, add the chopped onion, carrots, celery, and minced garlic. Sauté for about 5 minutes or until the vegetables begin to soften.

3. Deglaze with Chardonnay:
Pour in the Chardonnay wine and stir, scraping the bottom of the pot to release any browned bits. Allow it to simmer for a few minutes to cook off the alcohol.

4. Add Chicken and Broth:
Return the seared chicken to the pot. Pour in the chicken broth, add the bay leaves, and season with additional salt and black pepper if needed. Bring the mixture to a boil, then reduce the heat to low. Cover and simmer for about 20-25 minutes, or until the chicken is cooked through.

5. Prepare Dumpling Dough:
While the chicken is simmering, prepare the dumpling dough. In a mixing bowl, combine the all-purpose flour, baking powder, and salt. Add the cold, cubed butter and use a pastry cutter or fork to cut the butter into the dry ingredients until the mixture resembles coarse crumbs. Pour in the milk and stir until a soft dough forms.

6. Drop Dumplings:
Drop spoonfuls of dumpling dough onto the simmering chicken and broth. Cover the pot and let the dumplings cook for about 15 minutes, or until they are cooked through and no longer doughy in the center.

7. Serve:
Remove the bay leaves. Ladle into bowls, garnish with chopped fresh parsley if desired, and serve piping hot.

Notes

Chardonnay Shrimp and Grits

MAIN COURSE

Chardonnay Shrimp and Grits is a delightful Southern classic elevated with a touch of wine-inspired sophistication. Juicy shrimp are cooked in a creamy Chardonnay wine sauce and served over a bed of cheesy, creamy grits. Makes 4 servings.

Ingredients:

For the Shrimp:
- 1 lb large shrimp, peeled and deveined
- 2 tablespoons olive oil
- 1 onion, finely chopped
- 2 cloves garlic, minced
- 1/2 cup Chardonnay wine
- 1 cup heavy cream
- 2 tablespoons butter
- Salt and black pepper to taste
- Fresh parsley, chopped (for garnish)

For the Grits:
- 1 cup stone-ground grits
- 4 cups water
- 1 cup milk
- 1 cup shredded cheddar cheese
- 2 tablespoons butter
- Salt to taste

INSTRUCTIONS:

Prepare the Grits:

1. Boil Water and Milk: In a saucepan, bring the water and milk to a boil.

2. Add Grits: Slowly whisk in the grits, stirring constantly. Reduce the heat to low, cover, and simmer, stirring occasionally, for about 20-25 minutes, or until the grits are creamy and tender.

3. Stir in Cheese and Butter: Remove the saucepan from the heat and stir in the shredded cheddar cheese and butter until they are melted and well incorporated. Season with salt to taste. Cover to keep warm while you prepare the shrimp.

Prepare the Shrimp:

4. Sauté Onions and Garlic: In a large skillet, heat the olive oil over medium heat. Add the finely chopped onion and cook until it becomes translucent, about 3-4 minutes. Add the minced garlic and sauté for an additional 30 seconds.

5. Cook Shrimp: Add the peeled and deveined shrimp to the skillet and cook for 2-3 minutes on each side until they turn pink and opaque. Remove the shrimp from the skillet and set them aside.

6. Deglaze with Chardonnay: Pour the Chardonnay wine into the skillet, scraping any browned bits from the bottom of the pan. Let it simmer for a few minutes until it reduces by half.

7. Add Cream and Butter: Stir in the heavy cream and butter until the sauce thickens slightly, about 2-3 minutes. Season the sauce with salt and black pepper to taste.

8. Combine Shrimp and Sauce: Return the cooked shrimp to the skillet, coating them in the creamy Chardonnay sauce. Cook for an additional 2 minutes until the shrimp are heated through.

9. Serve: Spoon the creamy cheddar grits onto plates or shallow bowls. Top with Shrimp and Sauce. Garnish with chopped fresh parsley.

NOTES

Chardonnay Herbed-Crusted Cod

MAIN COURSE

Chardonnay Herbed-Crusted Cod with Pea Puree is a gourmet seafood dish that combines flaky cod fillets coated in a flavorful herb crust with a velvety Chardonnay-infused pea puree. It's a delightful and elegant recipe perfect for a special dinner. Makes 4 servings.

Ingredients:

For the Herbed-Crusted Cod:
- 4 cod fillets (6-8 ounces each)
- 1 cup breadcrumbs
- 2 tablespoons fresh parsley, finely chopped
- 2 tablespoons fresh dill, finely chopped
- Zest of 1 lemon
- 1/4 cup grated Parmesan cheese
- Salt and black pepper to taste
- 2 tablespoons olive oil
- 2 tablespoons Dijon mustard

For the Chardonnay Pea Puree:
- 2 cups fresh or frozen peas
- 1/2 cup Chardonnay wine
- 1/4 cup heavy cream
- 2 tablespoons unsalted butter
- Salt and black pepper to taste
- Fresh chives, chopped (for garnish)

INSTRUCTIONS:

Prepare the Herbed-Crusted Cod:

1. Preheat the Oven:
Preheat your oven to 400°F (200°C).

2. Make the Herb Crust:
In a mixing bowl, combine the breadcrumbs, finely chopped parsley, dill, lemon zest, grated Parmesan cheese, salt, and black pepper. Mix well.

3. Coat the Cod:
Brush each cod fillet with Dijon mustard, ensuring they are evenly coated. Press each fillet into the herb crumb mixture, pressing gently to adhere the crust.

4. Sear the Cod:
Heat the olive oil in an ovenproof skillet over medium-high heat. Place the cod fillets in the skillet and cook for 2-3 minutes on each side until the crust is golden brown.

5. Finish in the Oven:
Transfer the skillet to the preheated oven and bake for 5-7 minutes or until the cod is cooked through and flakes easily with a fork.

Prepare the Chardonnay Pea Puree:

6. Cook the Peas:
In a saucepan, bring the Chardonnay wine to a simmer. Add the peas and cook for about 3-4 minutes or until they are tender.

7. Make the Puree:
Using a slotted spoon, transfer the peas to a blender or food processor. Add the heavy cream and unsalted butter. Blend until the mixture is smooth and velvety. Season with salt and black pepper to taste.

8. Serve:
Spoon a generous portion of the pea puree onto each plate. Place a herbed-crusted cod fillet on top of the puree. Garnish with freshly chopped chives.

NOTES

Chardonnay Grilled Lobster

MAIN COURSE

Chardonnay Grilled Lobster is a luxurious seafood dish that features succulent lobster tails marinated in a flavorful Chardonnay wine sauce, then grilled to perfection. This dish embodies the perfect fusion of wine-infused sophistication and the smoky char of the grill. Makes 4 servings.

Ingredients:

For the Chardonnay Marinade:
- 1 cup Chardonnay wine
- 1/4 cup olive oil
- 3 cloves garlic, minced
- Zest and juice of 1 lemon
- 2 tablespoons fresh parsley, finely chopped
- Salt and black pepper to taste

For the Grilled Lobster:
- 4 lobster tails, shell-on
- 2 tablespoons melted butter
- Lemon wedges (for serving)
- Fresh parsley (for garnish)

Instructions:

Prepare the Chardonnay Marinade:

1. Mix Ingredients:
In a bowl, combine the Chardonnay wine, olive oil, minced garlic, lemon zest, lemon juice, finely chopped parsley, salt, and black pepper. Mix well to create the marinade.

Prepare the Lobster Tails:

2. Split the Lobster Tails:
Using kitchen shears or a sharp knife, carefully split the lobster tails in half lengthwise, keeping the shell intact. Gently open the shell without separating it from the meat.

3. Marinate the Lobster:
Place the split lobster tails in a large, shallow dish or a resealable plastic bag. Pour the Chardonnay marinade over the lobster tails, making sure they are well coated. Seal the bag or cover the dish and refrigerate for 30 minutes to 1 hour, allowing the flavors to infuse.

Grill the Lobster:

4. Preheat the Grill:
Preheat your grill to medium-high heat.

5. Brush with Butter:
Remove the lobster tails from the marinade and brush them with melted butter.

6. Grill the Lobster:
Place the lobster tails on the grill, shell side down. Grill for about 5-7 minutes, basting occasionally with more melted butter, until the lobster meat is opaque and slightly charred, and the shells turn bright red.

Serve:

7. Plate and Garnish:
Transfer the grilled lobster tails to a serving platter. Garnish with fresh parsley and serve with lemon wedges on the side.

Notes

Chardonnay Peach Cobbler

DESSERT

Chardonnay Peach Cobbler is a delightful dessert that marries the sweetness of ripe peaches with the subtle notes of Chardonnay wine. The tender, biscuit-like topping and warm, wine-infused peach filling create a harmonious and comforting treat. Makes 6-8 servings.

Ingredients:

For the Peach Filling:
- 6-8 ripe peaches, peeled, pitted, and sliced
- 1 cup Chardonnay wine
- 1/2 cup granulated sugar
- 1/4 cup brown sugar
- 1 teaspoon vanilla extract
- 1/2 teaspoon ground cinnamon
- 1/4 teaspoon ground nutmeg
- 2 tablespoons cornstarch

For the Biscuit Topping:
- 1 cup all-purpose flour
- 1/4 cup granulated sugar
- 1 1/2 teaspoons baking powder
- 1/2 teaspoon salt
- 1/2 cup unsalted butter, cold and cubed
- 1/4 cup Chardonnay wine
- 1/4 cup milk

INSTRUCTIONS:

Prepare the Peach Filling:

1. Combine Ingredients: In a large bowl, combine the sliced peaches, Chardonnay wine, granulated sugar, brown sugar, vanilla extract, ground cinnamon, ground nutmeg, and cornstarch. Gently toss until the peaches are evenly coated. Let the mixture sit while you prepare the topping.

Prepare the Biscuit Topping:

2. Mix Dry Ingredients: In a separate bowl, whisk together the flour, granulated sugar, baking powder, and salt.

3. Cut in Butter: Add the cold, cubed butter to the dry ingredients. Use a pastry cutter or your fingers to work the butter into the mixture until it resembles coarse crumbs.

4. Add Wine and Milk: Pour in the Chardonnay wine and milk. Stir until just combined; do not overmix. The dough will be slightly sticky.

Assemble and Bake:

5. Preheat Oven: Preheat your oven to 375°F (190°C).

6. Fill Baking Dish: Transfer the peach mixture to a greased 9x13-inch baking dish or a similar-sized ovenproof dish.

7. Drop the Dough: Using a spoon, drop spoonfuls of the biscuit dough evenly over the peaches.

8. Bake: Place the baking dish in the preheated oven and bake for 40-45 minutes, or until the topping is golden brown, and the peach filling is bubbling.

Serve:

9. Cool Slightly: Allow the cobbler to cool for a few minutes before serving. Serve warm with a scoop of vanilla ice cream or a dollop of whipped cream, if desired.

NOTES

Chardonnay Orange Soufflé

DESSERT

Chardonnay Orange Soufflé is a light and airy dessert that combines the bright, zesty flavors of oranges with the subtle sophistication of Chardonnay wine. This elegant soufflé is a delightful finish to any meal. Makes 4 servings.

Ingredients:

- 2 tablespoons unsalted butter, softened, for greasing the ramekins
- 1/2 cup granulated sugar, plus extra for coating the ramekins
- 3 large eggs, separated
- Zest of 2 oranges
- 1/2 cup freshly squeezed orange juice
- 1/4 cup Chardonnay wine
- 1/4 cup all-purpose flour
- 1/2 cup milk
- 1/4 teaspoon cream of tartar
- Pinch of salt
- Powdered sugar, for dusting

Instructions:

Preheat and Prepare:

1. Preheat Oven: Preheat your oven to 375°F (190°C). Place a baking sheet in the oven to heat as well.

2. Grease and Sugar Ramekins: Grease four 8-ounce ramekins with softened butter, then coat the insides with granulated sugar. Tap out any excess sugar.

Prepare Soufflé Base:

3. Beat Egg Yolks: In a mixing bowl, beat the egg yolks with 1/4 cup of granulated sugar until the mixture is pale and slightly thickened.

4. Add Orange Zest and Juice: Stir in the orange zest, freshly squeezed orange juice, and Chardonnay wine.

5. Add Flour and Milk: Gradually add the flour and milk, alternating between the two until fully incorporated. The mixture should be smooth.

Whip Egg Whites:

6. Beat Egg Whites: In a separate clean, dry bowl, beat the egg whites until they become foamy. Add a pinch of salt and the cream of tartar. Continue beating until soft peaks form.

Fold and Bake:

7. Fold in Egg Whites: Gently fold the beaten egg whites into the orange mixture until no white streaks remain. Be careful not to deflate the egg whites.

8. Fill Ramekins: Divide the soufflé mixture among the prepared ramekins, filling them almost to the top.

9. Bake: Place the filled ramekins on the preheated baking sheet in the oven. Bake for about 20-25 minutes or until the soufflés have risen and are golden brown on top.

10. Serve: Remove from the oven and dust the tops with powdered sugar. Serve immediately while the soufflés are puffed and airy. They can be garnished with a twist of orange peel or a dollop of whipped cream, if desired.

Notes

MERLOT
Wine Notes

~ Food Pairing Suggestions ~

Red Meats: Merlot's soft tannins and fruit-forward character make it an excellent match for red meats like beef, lamb, and venison.

Roasted Poultry: It pairs well with roasted or grilled chicken, duck, or turkey.

Pasta: Merlot complements pasta dishes, especially those with tomato-based sauces or meat ragù.

Mild Cheeses: Try it with soft to semi-soft cheeses like brie or camembert.

Mushroom Dishes: Its earthy notes harmonize with mushroom-based dishes, such as risotto or mushroom stroganoff.

Burgers: Merlot's approachable nature makes it a great choice for pairing with burgers, including veggie burgers.

Herb-Seasoned Dishes: Herbs like thyme and rosemary enhance Merlot's flavor profile, making it a good match for dishes seasoned with these herbs.

Charcuterie: Enjoy Merlot with a charcuterie board featuring cured meats and a variety of cheeses.

Grilled Vegetables: Merlot's softer tannins can complement the smokiness of grilled vegetables like eggplant and bell peppers.

Chocolate Desserts: Its fruitiness makes it a pleasant pairing with dark chocolate desserts or chocolate-covered strawberries.

PRIMARY FLAVORS
~

Fruit Notes:
Red and black fruit flavors like plum, cherry, and raspberry.

Herbaceous Notes:
Green bell pepper, mint, and sometimes a hint of eucalyptus.

Spices:
Often features notes of baking spices such as cinnamon and clove.

Oak Influence:
Depending on aging, you may detect vanilla, cedar, or toast.

TASTE PROFILE
~

Body:
Medium to full-bodied, depending on the region and winemaking style.

Acidity:
Moderate, providing balance.

Tannins:
Generally soft and approachable.

Alcohol:
Moderate.

Finish:
Smooth, with a medium to long finish, sometimes with a velvety texture.

Chapter Three
Merlot

Prepare to embark on a culinary journey that celebrates the marvel of Merlot wine, a varietal cherished not only for its velvety sips but also for its exceptional ability to transform ordinary dishes into extraordinary masterpieces.

Merlot, often described as the "people's wine," boasts qualities that set it apart as an ideal companion in the kitchen. In this chapter, we delve into the multifaceted world of Merlot, uncovering the secrets of its remarkable flavor profile and its unique capacity to harmonize with a wide array of ingredients.

With its plush notes of ripe plum, cherry, and subtle herbal accents, Merlot offers a harmonious balance that complements a plethora of culinary creations. Whether you're crafting a comforting beef stew, searing a succulent duck breast, or indulging in a decadent chocolate dessert, Merlot's versatility knows no bounds.

Join us in exploring Merlot's nuanced flavors, its characteristic soft tannins, and its inviting aroma that beckons with every swirl. Discover how this varietal can become your culinary muse, transforming your kitchen into a haven of flavors and aromas that delight the senses.

Merlot Kalimotxo

COCKTAIL

The Merlot Kalimotxo is a simple yet intriguing cocktail that combines the robust richness of Merlot wine with the zesty refreshment of cola. It's a classic Basque Country favorite, perfect for cooling down on a hot day or enjoying a unique and easy-to-make beverage. Makes one glass, easily scalable for multiple servings.

Ingredients:

- 4 oz Merlot wine
- 4 oz cola (use your favorite brand)
- Ice cubes
- Lemon or lime wedge for garnish (optional)

Instructions:

1. Chill Your Glass:
Fill a highball glass with ice cubes to chill.

2. Prepare the Cocktail:
In the chilled glass, pour in the Merlot wine, followed by the cola.

3. Stir Gently:
Give the mixture a gentle stir to combine the wine and cola.

4. Garnish:
If you like, garnish your Merlot Kalimotxo with a lemon or lime wedge.

5. Enjoy:
Sip and savor this unique and refreshing blend of Merlot's richness and cola's fizz. It's a great choice for casual gatherings, picnics, or as a fun alternative to traditional wine or cocktails.

Notes

Merlot Mary
COCKTAIL

The Merlot Mary is a bold and savory twist on the classic Bloody Mary, incorporating the robust richness of Merlot wine alongside the traditional tomato and spice flavors. It's a unique and satisfying cocktail that's perfect for those who enjoy a little extra depth in their drinks. Makes one cocktail, easily scalable for multiple servings.

Ingredients:

- 1 1/2 oz Merlot wine
- 3 oz tomato juice
- 1/2 oz vodka
- 1/2 oz fresh lemon juice
- 1 dash hot sauce (adjust to taste)
- 1 dash Worcestershire sauce
- Pinch of salt and black pepper
- Ice cubes
- Lemon wedge and celery stalk for garnish
- Optional garnishes: olives, pickles, or a slice of bacon

Instructions:

1. Chill Your Glass:
Fill a tall glass with ice cubes to chill.

2. Prepare the Cocktail:
In the chilled glass, combine the Merlot wine, tomato juice, vodka, fresh lemon juice, hot sauce, Worcestershire sauce, salt, and black pepper. Stir gently to mix.

3. Garnish:
Garnish your Merlot Mary with a lemon wedge and a celery stalk. Feel free to add additional garnishes like olives, pickles, or even a slice of bacon if you like.

4. Enjoy:
Sip and savor this intriguing and savory twist on the classic Bloody Mary. The Merlot wine adds a layer of depth and complexity to the familiar flavors, making it a delightful choice for brunch or whenever you're in the mood for a bold cocktail.

Notes

Merlot Sausage Rolls

APPETIZER

Merlot Wine Sausage Rolls are a delectable combination of savory sausage, flaky pastry, and the rich, fruity essence of Merlot wine. These bite-sized appetizers are perfect for parties or as a tasty snack. Makes 8 servings.

Ingredients:

For the Sausage Filling:
- 1 pound ground sausage (pork or beef)
- 1/4 cup finely chopped onion
- 1/4 cup finely chopped bell pepper
- 1/4 cup finely chopped mushrooms
- 1 clove garlic, minced
- 1/4 cup Merlot wine
- Salt and black pepper to taste
- 1 tablespoon olive oil

For the Pastry:
- 1 sheet puff pastry, thawed
- 1 egg, beaten (for egg wash)

INSTRUCTIONS:

Prepare the Sausage Filling:

1. Sauté Vegetables: In a skillet, heat the olive oil over medium heat. Add the chopped onion, bell pepper, mushrooms, and garlic. Sauté until the vegetables are softened.

2. Add Sausage: Add the ground sausage to the skillet. Break it up with a spatula and cook until browned.

3. Deglaze with Merlot: Pour in the Merlot wine and stir to deglaze the pan, scraping up any browned bits from the bottom. Cook for a few minutes until most of the wine has evaporated. Season with salt and black pepper to taste. Remove from heat and let the filling cool.

Assemble the Sausage Rolls:

4. Preheat Oven: Preheat your oven to 375°F (190°C) and line a baking sheet with parchment paper.

5. Roll Out Pastry: Roll out the thawed puff pastry on a lightly floured surface to create a rectangle.

6. Cut into Strips: Cut the pastry into 8 equal strips.

7. Fill and Roll: Place a portion of the cooled sausage filling along the length of each pastry strip. Roll the pastry around the filling, sealing the seam with a bit of beaten egg. Place the rolls seam-side down on the prepared baking sheet.

8. Brush with Egg Wash: Brush the tops of the sausage rolls with beaten egg to give them a golden finish.

Bake and Serve:

9. Bake: Bake the Merlot Wine Sausage Rolls in the preheated oven for about 20-25 minutes or until they are puffed and golden brown.

10. Cool and Serve: Allow the sausage rolls to cool slightly before serving. They can be enjoyed warm or at room temperature.

NOTES

Merlot Buffalo Chicken Biscuits

APPETIZER

Merlot Wine Buffalo Chicken Biscuits are a delightful fusion of tender, spicy chicken and buttery biscuits, elevated with a splash of Merlot wine. These bite-sized treats are perfect for game day or any casual gathering. Makes 6 servings.

Ingredients:

For the Buffalo Chicken:
- 2 cups cooked chicken, shredded (rotisserie chicken works well)
- 1/2 cup buffalo sauce
- 2 tablespoons unsalted butter, melted
- 1/4 cup Merlot wine
- Salt and black pepper to taste
- 1/4 cup chopped green onions (for garnish)

For the Biscuits:
- 1 can (16.3 ounces) refrigerated biscuits (8 count)

INSTRUCTIONS:

Prepare the Buffalo Chicken:

1. Combine Ingredients: In a mixing bowl, combine the shredded cooked chicken, buffalo sauce, melted butter, Merlot wine, salt, and black pepper. Mix until the chicken is well coated with the sauce.

2. Heat Chicken: Transfer the mixture to a skillet and cook over medium heat for about 5-7 minutes, stirring occasionally, until the chicken is heated through and the sauce has thickened slightly.

3. Garnish: Remove the skillet from heat and sprinkle the chopped green onions over the buffalo chicken. Set aside.

Bake the Biscuits:

4. Preheat Oven: Preheat your oven according to the biscuit package instructions.

5. Bake Biscuits: Place the refrigerated biscuits on a baking sheet lined with parchment paper and bake them as directed until they are golden brown.

Assemble the Merlot Wine Buffalo Chicken Biscuits:

6. Slice Biscuits: Let the baked biscuits cool slightly, then slice each one in half horizontally.

7. Add Buffalo Chicken: Spoon a generous portion of the buffalo chicken mixture onto the bottom half of each biscuit.

8. Top and Serve: Place the top half of the biscuit over the chicken mixture to create a sandwich. Secure each with a toothpick. Serve immediately as a scrumptious appetizer.

NOTES

Merlot Green Bean Casserole

SIDE DISH

Merlot Wine Green Bean Casserole is a delightful twist on a classic favorite. Tender green beans are smothered in a creamy Merlot wine-infused sauce and topped with crispy fried onions for a perfect side dish. Makes 8 servings.

Ingredients:

- 1 1/2 pounds fresh green beans, trimmed and blanched
- 1/4 cup unsalted butter
- 1/4 cup all-purpose flour
- 1 cup Merlot wine
- 1 cup chicken or vegetable broth
- 1 cup heavy cream
- 1 teaspoon garlic powder
- 1 teaspoon onion powder
- Salt and black pepper to taste
- 1 1/2 cups crispy fried onions (store-bought or homemade)

INSTRUCTIONS:

1. Prepare the Green Beans:
Bring a large pot of salted water to a boil. Add the green beans and blanch them for about 3-4 minutes until they are bright green and slightly tender. Drain and immediately transfer them to an ice water bath to stop the cooking process. Drain again and set aside.

2. Make the Merlot Wine Sauce:
In a large skillet, melt the unsalted butter over medium heat. Add the flour and whisk continuously for about 1-2 minutes to create a roux. Slowly pour in the Merlot wine while continuing to whisk. Cook for another 2-3 minutes, allowing the wine to reduce and the mixture to thicken. Gradually add the chicken or vegetable broth, heavy cream, garlic powder, onion powder, salt, and black pepper. Continue to whisk until the sauce is smooth and thickened. Remove from heat.

3. Combine Green Beans and Sauce:
In a large mixing bowl, gently fold the blanched green beans into the Merlot wine sauce, ensuring they are well coated.

4. Transfer to a Baking Dish:
Preheat your oven to 350°F (175°C). Transfer the green bean mixture into a greased 9x13-inch baking dish, spreading it out evenly.

5. Bake:
Cover the baking dish with foil and bake in the preheated oven for 25-30 minutes, or until the green bean casserole is hot and bubbling.

6. Add Crispy Fried Onions:
Remove the foil and sprinkle the crispy fried onions evenly over the top of the casserole.

7. Broil:
Switch the oven to broil and place the casserole under the broiler for 1-2 minutes, or until the fried onions are golden brown and crispy. Watch closely to prevent burning.

8. Serve:
Remove from the oven and let it cool slightly before serving.

NOTES

Merlot Zucchini Parmesan

SIDE DISH

Merlot Wine Zucchini Parmesan is a delectable Italian-inspired dish that combines tender zucchini slices with a rich Merlot-infused tomato sauce and layers of melted cheese. It's a comforting and flavorful side dish or vegetarian main course. Makes 4-6 servings.

Ingredients:

- 4 medium-sized zucchini, sliced into 1/4-inch rounds
- 2 tablespoons olive oil
- 1 onion, finely chopped
- 3 cloves garlic, minced
- 1 (14-ounce) can crushed tomatoes
- 1/2 cup Merlot wine
- 1 teaspoon dried basil
- 1 teaspoon dried oregano
- Salt and black pepper to taste
- 1 cup shredded mozzarella cheese
- 1/2 cup grated Parmesan cheese
- Fresh basil leaves for garnish (optional)

Instructions:

1. Preheat the Oven:
Preheat your oven to 375°F (190°C).

2. Sauté the Zucchini:
In a large skillet, heat the olive oil over medium heat. Add the zucchini slices and sauté them for about 2-3 minutes per side until they are lightly browned and tender. Remove the zucchini from the skillet and set it aside.

3. Prepare the Merlot Tomato Sauce:
In the same skillet, add the chopped onion and minced garlic. Sauté for 2-3 minutes until they are translucent and fragrant. Pour in the crushed tomatoes and Merlot wine. Stir in the dried basil, dried oregano, salt, and black pepper. Simmer the sauce for about 10 minutes, allowing it to thicken and the flavors to meld.

4. Layer the Zucchini Parmesan:
In a greased baking dish, start by spreading a thin layer of the Merlot tomato sauce. Add a layer of sautéed zucchini slices on top of the sauce. Sprinkle a portion of mozzarella cheese and Parmesan cheese over the zucchini. Repeat these layers until you use up all the zucchini, ending with a layer of cheese on top.

5. Bake:
Cover the baking dish with aluminum foil and bake in the preheated oven for 20-25 minutes or until the cheese is bubbly and golden.

6. Broil (Optional):
If you desire a crispy, golden top, you can uncover the dish and place it under the broiler for 1-2 minutes, keeping a close eye to prevent burning.

7. Serve:
Remove from the oven and let it cool slightly. Garnish with fresh basil leaves if desired.

Notes

Merlot Sloppy Joes

MAIN COURSE

Merlot Wine Sloppy Joes are a gourmet twist on a classic comfort food favorite. Ground beef simmered in a rich Merlot wine and tomato sauce, served on toasted buns with a zesty slaw, making for a hearty and satisfying meal. Makes 4-6 servings.

Ingredients:

For the Sloppy Joes:
- 1 lb ground beef
- 1 onion, finely chopped
- 2 cloves garlic, minced
- 1/2 cup Merlot wine
- 1 (14-ounce) can crushed tomatoes
- 2 tablespoons tomato paste
- 2 tablespoons brown sugar
- 1 tablespoon Worcestershire sauce
- 1 teaspoon Dijon mustard
- Salt and black pepper to taste
- 4-6 hamburger buns, toasted

For the Zesty Slaw:
- 2 cups cabbage, thinly sliced
- 1 carrot, grated
- 1/4 cup mayonnaise
- 1 tablespoon white vinegar
- 1 teaspoon sugar
- Salt and black pepper to taste

INSTRUCTIONS:

1. Brown the Ground Beef:
In a large skillet over medium-high heat, cook the ground beef until it's browned and crumbled. Drain any excess fat.

2. Sauté the Aromatics:
Add the chopped onion and minced garlic to the skillet with the cooked beef. Sauté for 2-3 minutes until the onion is translucent and fragrant.

3. Deglaze with Merlot Wine:
Pour in the Merlot wine and allow it to simmer for 2-3 minutes, scraping up any browned bits from the bottom of the skillet.

4. Create the Tomato Sauce:
Stir in the crushed tomatoes, tomato paste, brown sugar, Worcestershire sauce, and Dijon mustard. Season with salt and black pepper to taste. Reduce the heat to low and let the sauce simmer for 15-20 minutes, allowing the flavors to meld and the sauce to thicken. Add a bit of water if it gets too thick.

5. Prepare the Zesty Slaw:
In a mixing bowl, combine the thinly sliced cabbage and grated carrot. In a separate bowl, whisk together the mayonnaise, white vinegar, sugar, salt, and black pepper. Pour this dressing over the cabbage and carrot mixture, tossing to coat. Refrigerate until ready to use.

6. Assemble the Merlot Wine Sloppy Joes:
Toast the hamburger buns until they are lightly browned. Spoon a generous portion of the Merlot wine-infused beef mixture onto each toasted bun. Top with a generous helping of zesty slaw.

7. Serve:
Serve hot, accompanied by your favorite sides.

NOTES

Merlot Chili Mac

MAIN COURSE

Merlot Wine Chili Mac is a hearty and flavorful dish that combines the bold richness of Merlot wine with classic chili and macaroni. It's the perfect comfort food for a cozy evening in. Makes 6-8 servings.

Ingredients:

- 1 lb ground beef
- 1 onion, chopped
- 2 cloves garlic, minced
- 1/2 cup Merlot wine
- 1 (14-ounce) can diced tomatoes
- 1 (14-ounce) can kidney beans, drained and rinsed
- 1 (14-ounce) can black beans, drained and rinsed
- 2 cups beef broth
- 1 cup elbow macaroni
- 2 tablespoons chili powder (adjust to your spice preference)
- 1 teaspoon cumin
- Salt and black pepper to taste
- 1 cup shredded cheddar cheese
- Chopped fresh cilantro and sour cream for garnish (optional)

Instructions:

1. Brown the Ground Beef:
In a large pot or Dutch oven over medium-high heat, cook the ground beef until it's browned and crumbled. Drain any excess fat.

2. Sauté the Aromatics:
Add the chopped onion and minced garlic to the pot with the cooked beef. Sauté for 2-3 minutes until the onion is translucent and fragrant.

3. Deglaze with Merlot Wine:
Pour in the Merlot wine and allow it to simmer for 2-3 minutes, scraping up any browned bits from the bottom of the pot.

4. Add Tomatoes and Beans:
Stir in the diced tomatoes, kidney beans, and black beans.

5. Season and Simmer:
Add the beef broth, chili powder, cumin, salt, and black pepper. Stir to combine.
Bring the mixture to a boil, then reduce the heat to low. Let it simmer uncovered for about 15 minutes, allowing the flavors to meld.

6. Cook the Macaroni:
While the chili is simmering, cook the elbow macaroni separately according to the package instructions until al dente. Drain and set aside.

7. Combine the Chili and Macaroni:
Stir the cooked macaroni into the chili mixture. Let it simmer together for an additional 5-10 minutes.

8. Serve:
Ladle into bowls, garnish with shredded cheddar cheese, chopped fresh cilantro, and a dollop of sour cream if desired.

Notes

Merlot Turkey Chili

MAIN COURSE

Slow Cooker Merlot Turkey Chili is a hearty and flavorful dish that combines lean ground turkey with the rich depth of Merlot wine. Let your slow cooker do the work, and come home to a comforting bowl of chili. Makes 6-8 servings.

Ingredients:

- 1 lb lean ground turkey
- 1 onion, chopped
- 2 cloves garlic, minced
- 1 red bell pepper, chopped
- 1 yellow bell pepper, chopped
- 1 (14-ounce) can diced tomatoes
- 1 (14-ounce) can kidney beans, drained and rinsed
- 1 (14-ounce) can black beans, drained and rinsed
- 1 cup Merlot wine
- 2 cups beef broth
- 2 tablespoons chili powder (adjust to your spice preference)
- 1 teaspoon cumin
- Salt and black pepper to taste
- 1 cup frozen corn kernels
- Shredded cheddar cheese and chopped green onions for garnish (optional)

INSTRUCTIONS:

1. Brown the Turkey:
In a large skillet over medium-high heat, cook the ground turkey until it's browned and no longer pink. Break it apart with a spoon as it cooks. Drain any excess fat.

2. Sauté the Aromatics:
In the same skillet, add the chopped onion, minced garlic, and both chopped bell peppers. Sauté for 2-3 minutes until the onion is translucent and the peppers are slightly softened.

3. Transfer to Slow Cooker:
Transfer the cooked turkey and sautéed vegetables to your slow cooker.

4. Add Tomatoes, Beans, and Merlot:
Add the diced tomatoes, kidney beans, black beans, and Merlot wine to the slow cooker.

5. Season and Cook:
Pour in the beef broth, and season with chili powder, cumin, salt, and black pepper. Stir to combine all ingredients. Cover the slow cooker and cook on low for 6-8 hours or on high for 3-4 hours.

6. Add Corn and Serve:
About 30 minutes before serving, stir in the frozen corn kernels. Serve hot, garnished with shredded cheddar cheese and chopped green onions if desired.

NOTES

Merlot Chicken-Fried Steak

MAIN COURSE

Merlot Wine-Infused Chicken-Fried Steak is a Southern classic with a sophisticated twist. Tender cube steak is marinated in Merlot wine, breaded, and fried to golden perfection, then smothered in a rich Merlot gravy. Makes 4 servings.

Ingredients:

For the Marinated Steak:
- 4 cube steaks
- 1 cup Merlot wine
- Salt and black pepper to taste

For the Breading:
- 1 cup all-purpose flour
- 1 teaspoon paprika
- 1/2 teaspoon garlic powder
- 1/2 teaspoon onion powder
- Salt and black pepper to taste
- 2 eggs, beaten
- Vegetable oil for frying

For the Merlot Gravy:
- 2 tablespoons butter
- 2 tablespoons all-purpose flour
- 1 cup Merlot wine
- 1 cup beef broth
- Salt and black pepper to taste

INSTRUCTIONS:

1. Marinate the Steak:
Place the cube steaks in a shallow dish, season with salt and black pepper, and pour the Merlot wine over them. Cover and refrigerate for at least 2 hours or overnight.

2. Prepare the Breading:
In a shallow bowl, combine the flour, paprika, garlic powder, onion powder, salt, and black pepper. In another bowl, beat the eggs.

3. Bread the Steaks:
Remove the cube steaks from the marinade and allow excess liquid to drain. Dip each steak into the flour mixture, coating both sides. Dip the floured steak into the beaten eggs, allowing excess to drip off. Return the steak to the flour mixture, coating evenly. Press the flour mixture onto the steak to adhere.

4. Fry the Steaks:
In a large skillet, heat about 1/4 inch of vegetable oil over medium-high heat. Carefully add the breaded steaks to the hot oil and fry until golden brown on each side, about 3-4 minutes per side. Remove and drain on paper towels.

5. Make the Merlot Gravy:
In the same skillet, discard most of the oil, leaving about 2 tablespoons. Add the butter and let it melt. Sprinkle in the flour and whisk continuously for about 2 minutes until it turns a light golden brown. Gradually pour in the Merlot wine and beef broth, stirring constantly until the mixture thickens. Season with salt and black pepper.

6. Serve:
Pour the Merlot gravy over the chicken-fried steaks. Serve hot, accompanied by your choice of sides, such as mashed potatoes and greens.

NOTES

Merlot Bread Pudding

DESSERT

Merlot Wine-Infused Bread Pudding is a delightful dessert that combines the richness of Merlot wine with the comforting warmth of bread pudding. This indulgent treat is perfect for satisfying your sweet cravings. Makes 6 servings.

Ingredients:

For the Bread Pudding:
- 4 cups stale bread, cubed
- 2 cups whole milk
- 1 cup Merlot wine
- 3/4 cup granulated sugar
- 3 large eggs
- 1 teaspoon vanilla extract
- 1/2 teaspoon ground cinnamon
- 1/4 teaspoon ground nutmeg
- 1/4 cup raisins (optional)
- 1/4 cup chopped pecans (optional)

For the Merlot Wine Sauce:
- 1/2 cup Merlot wine
- 1/4 cup granulated sugar
- 1/4 cup unsalted butter
- 1/4 cup heavy cream
- 1/2 teaspoon vanilla extract
- A pinch of salt

INSTRUCTIONS:

1. Prepare the Bread Cubes:
Cut the stale bread into bite-sized cubes. You can use French bread, brioche, or any bread of your choice. Stale bread works best as it absorbs the custard mixture well.

2. Mix the Custard:
In a mixing bowl, combine the whole milk, Merlot wine, granulated sugar, eggs, vanilla extract, ground cinnamon, and ground nutmeg. Whisk until the mixture is well combined.

3. Soak the Bread:
Place the bread cubes in a separate large bowl. Pour the custard mixture over the bread cubes. Add raisins and chopped pecans if desired. Gently stir to ensure the bread is evenly coated. Let it sit for about 15-20 minutes, allowing the bread to absorb the liquid.

4. Preheat the Oven:
Preheat your oven to 350°F (175°C).

5. Bake the Pudding:
Grease a baking dish or individual ramekins. Transfer the soaked bread mixture into the dish or ramekins. Place the baking dish or ramekins in a larger baking pan. Fill the larger pan with hot water until it reaches halfway up the sides of the smaller dish or ramekins. This creates a water bath, ensuring even baking and a creamy texture. Bake for 40-45 minutes or until the pudding is set and the top is golden brown.

6. Make the Merlot Wine Sauce:
While the pudding is baking, prepare the Merlot wine sauce. In a saucepan, combine the Merlot wine and granulated sugar. Bring to a simmer and let it cook for about 5 minutes or until it reduces slightly. Add the butter, heavy cream, vanilla extract, and a pinch of salt. Stir until the sauce thickens. Remove from heat.

7. Serve:
Once the bread pudding is done, remove it from the oven. Drizzle the warm Merlot wine sauce over the top. Serve as is or with a scoop of vanilla ice cream for an extra treat.

NOTES

Merlot Pineapple Upside-Down Cake

DESSERT

Elevate the classic Pineapple Upside-Down Cake by infusing it with the rich and fruity flavors of Merlot wine. This dessert is a delightful twist on a beloved classic. Makes 8 servings.

Ingredients:

For the Pineapple Layer:
- 1/4 cup (1/2 stick) unsalted butter
- 3/4 cup packed brown sugar
- 7-8 pineapple rings (canned or fresh)
- Maraschino cherries (optional)

For the Cake Batter:
- 1 1/2 cups all-purpose flour
- 1 1/2 teaspoons baking powder
- 1/2 teaspoon salt
- 1/2 cup (1 stick) unsalted butter, softened
- 1 cup granulated sugar
- 2 large eggs
- 1 teaspoon vanilla extract
- 1/2 cup Merlot wine
- 1/2 cup whole milk

INSTRUCTIONS:

1. Prepare the Pineapple Layer:
Preheat your oven to 350°F (175°C). In a 9-inch round cake pan, melt 1/4 cup of butter over low heat. Remove from heat and sprinkle the brown sugar evenly over the melted butter. Arrange the pineapple rings on top of the brown sugar. You can also place a maraschino cherry in the center of each pineapple ring if desired.

2. Make the Cake Batter:
In a mixing bowl, whisk together the flour, baking powder, and salt. Set aside. In another mixing bowl, cream together the softened butter and granulated sugar until light and fluffy. Beat in the eggs one at a time, then stir in the vanilla extract. Gradually add the dry ingredients, alternating with the Merlot wine and milk, beginning and ending with the dry ingredients. Mix until just combined.

3. Layer and Bake:
Carefully spread the cake batter over the pineapple layer in the cake pan, making sure it's evenly distributed.

4. Bake:
Bake in the preheated oven for 40-45 minutes or until a toothpick inserted into the center comes out clean.

5. Cool and Invert:
Allow the cake to cool in the pan for about 10 minutes. Then, place a serving plate on top of the cake pan and invert it. Carefully lift off the cake pan.

6. Serve:
Enjoy it warm, and admire the beautiful pineapple topping.

NOTES

ZINFANDEL
Wine Notes

~ Food Pairing Suggestions ~

Grilled Meats: Zinfandel's bold flavors and moderate tannins make it an excellent choice for grilled meats like ribs, sausages, and burgers.

Barbecue: Its smoky and spicy notes complement the flavors of barbecue dishes, including pulled pork, smoked brisket, and grilled chicken with spicy rubs or sauces.

Spicy Cuisine: Zinfandel's fruitiness can temper the heat in spicy dishes like Mexican or Cajun cuisine.

Hard Cheeses: Pair Zinfandel with hard cheeses like aged cheddar or pecorino.

Pizza: The wine's fruit-forward character and acidity make it a delightful partner for pizza, especially those with meat toppings and tomato sauce.

Mediterranean Cuisine: Try it with Mediterranean dishes like lamb kebabs, moussaka, or eggplant Parmesan.

Pasta with Tomato-Based Sauces: Zinfandel's acidity complements tomato-based pasta dishes, including spaghetti bolognese.

Grilled Vegetables: Its fruitiness pairs well with grilled vegetables like bell peppers, eggplant, and zucchini.

Chocolate Desserts: Zinfandel's jammy qualities can harmonize with chocolate desserts, especially those with dark chocolate and berry components.

PRIMARY FLAVORS
~

Fruit Notes:
Dark fruit flavors such as blackberry, black cherry, and sometimes raspberry or plum.

Spices:
Often features notes of black pepper, baking spices like cinnamon and clove, and sometimes a hint of licorice.

Jammy Characteristics:
Zinfandel can exhibit jammy qualities, especially in warmer climates, akin to fruit preserves or compote.

Oak Influence:
Depending on aging, you may detect vanilla, toast, or even caramel.

TASTE PROFILE
~

Body:
Typically medium to full-bodied, but it can vary widely based on the winemaking style.

Acidity:
Moderate to high, offering a refreshing quality.

Tannins:
Generally moderate to soft, although some Zinfandels can have firmer tannins.

Alcohol:
Often higher in alcohol content compared to many other red wines.

Finish:
Can be smooth and medium to long, with a touch of spice.

Chapter Four
Zinfandel

Welcome to a culinary journey that celebrates Zinfandel wine, a varietal that wears many hats in the world of cuisine. Beyond its reputation as a bold and expressive wine, Zinfandel reveals a secret talent when it steps into the kitchen.

In this chapter, we'll explore the multifaceted qualities of Zinfandel and unlock its potential as a culinary muse. From its vibrant flavors of dark berries and spicy nuances to its welcoming embrace of diverse ingredients, Zinfandel is the perfect companion for those seeking culinary adventure.

Zinfandel's characteristic charm lies in its ability to complement an array of dishes, from smoky barbecue ribs to zesty Mediterranean fare. With its robust fruitiness and spicy personality, it transforms ordinary meals into extraordinary experiences.

Join us as we delve into the heart of Zinfandel's flavor profile, characterized by blackberry and black cherry notes, a touch of black pepper, and a hint of jammy richness. Through these recipes and techniques, you'll learn how to harness Zinfandel's culinary prowess, elevating your dishes to a symphony of flavors that dance on the palate.

Zinfandel Lemonade Fizz

COCKTAIL

The Zinfandel Lemonade Fizz is a delightful and refreshing cocktail that combines the fruity zing of Zinfandel wine with the bright, tangy flavors of lemonade. It's a perfect fusion of wine and citrus, making it ideal for sunny afternoons or as a sparkling aperitif. Makes one cocktail, easily scalable for multiple servings.

Ingredients:

- 2 oz Zinfandel wine
- 4 oz lemonade (homemade or store-bought)
- 1 oz club soda or sparkling water
- 1/2 oz simple syrup (adjust to taste)
- Ice cubes
- Lemon wheel or twist for garnish (optional)

INSTRUCTIONS:

1. Chill Your Glass:
Fill a tall glass with ice cubes to chill.

2. Prepare the Cocktail:
In the chilled glass, combine the Zinfandel wine, lemonade, club soda or sparkling water, and simple syrup. Stir gently to mix.

3. Garnish:
If desired, garnish your Zinfandel Lemonade Fizz with a lemon wheel or twist.

4. Enjoy:
Sip and savor this delightful cocktail that marries the fruity charm of Zinfandel wine with the zesty allure of lemonade. It's a fantastic choice for picnics, poolside relaxation, or as a prelude to a summer evening.

NOTES

Zinfandel Amaretto Bliss

COCKTAIL

The Zinfandel Amaretto Bliss is a harmonious cocktail that combines the bold flavors of Zinfandel wine with the sweet, nutty notes of Amaretto liqueur. It's a delightful fusion of tastes for those who appreciate the rich and the indulgent. Makes one cocktail, easily scalable for multiple servings.

Ingredients:

- 2 oz Zinfandel wine
- 1 oz Amaretto liqueur
- 1/2 oz fresh lemon juice
- 1/4 oz simple syrup (adjust to taste)
- Lemon twist or a maraschino cherry for garnish (optional)
- Ice cubes

Instructions:

1. Chill Your Glass:
Place a stemmed wine glass or rocks glass in the freezer to chill.

2. Prepare the Cocktail:
In a shaker filled with ice, combine the Zinfandel wine, Amaretto liqueur, fresh lemon juice, and simple syrup.

3. Shake Vigorously:
Shake the mixture vigorously for about 10-15 seconds. This chills the ingredients and ensures proper blending.

4. Strain and Serve:
Remove the chilled glass from the freezer and strain the cocktail into it.

5. Garnish:
If desired, garnish your Zinfandel Amaretto Bliss with a twist of lemon peel or a maraschino cherry.

6. Enjoy:
Sip and savor this blissful fusion of flavors that combines the bold character of Zinfandel wine with the nutty sweetness of Amaretto. It's a delightful choice for those who appreciate a harmonious and indulgent cocktail.

Notes

Zinfandel Bacon Jalapeño Poppers

APPETIZER

Zinfandel Wine Bacon Jalapeño Poppers are the perfect combination of heat and savory flavors. Stuffed with a zesty cream cheese mixture and wrapped in crispy bacon, these poppers are elevated with a Zinfandel wine glaze, making them an irresistible appetizer. Makes 6-8 servings.

Ingredients:

For the Jalapeño Poppers:
- 12 large jalapeño peppers, halved lengthwise and seeded
- 8 ounces cream cheese, softened
- 1 cup shredded cheddar cheese
- 1 clove garlic, minced
- Salt and black pepper to taste
- 12 slices bacon, cut in half crosswise

For the Zinfandel Wine Glaze:
- 1 cup Zinfandel wine
- 1/4 cup brown sugar
- 2 tablespoons balsamic vinegar
- 1/2 teaspoon red pepper flakes (adjust to your heat preference)

INSTRUCTIONS:

1. Prepare the Jalapeño Poppers:
In a mixing bowl, combine the softened cream cheese, shredded cheddar cheese, minced garlic, salt, and black pepper. Mix until all ingredients are well incorporated.

2. Stuff the Jalapeños:
Spoon the cream cheese mixture into each jalapeño half, filling them evenly.

3. Wrap with Bacon:
Wrap each stuffed jalapeño half with a half-slice of bacon, securing it with a toothpick.

4. Bake the Poppers:
Preheat your oven to 375°F (190°C). Place the bacon-wrapped jalapeños on a baking sheet lined with parchment paper. Bake for about 25-30 minutes or until the bacon is crispy and the jalapeños are tender.

5. Make the Zinfandel Wine Glaze:
While the poppers are baking, combine the Zinfandel wine, brown sugar, balsamic vinegar, and red pepper flakes in a saucepan. Bring the mixture to a boil, then reduce the heat and simmer for about 15-20 minutes, or until the glaze thickens and reduces by half.

6. Glaze the Poppers:
Once the poppers are done baking, remove them from the oven and brush each one generously with the Zinfandel wine glaze.

7. Serve:
Arrange on a serving platter and serve them hot as a delectable appetizer.

NOTES

GUEST RECIPE

Zinfandel Brandied Mushroom Paté

APPETIZER

"I can't say enough about how delicious this paté is – a real hit at all parties. I think it's the brandy, my addition to the original recipe." ~ S. Elaine Lyttleton, The Chinook Cook, Hatfield Creek Vineyard & Winery

Ingredients:

1/4 cup Butter
1 lb. Mushrooms finely chopped, stems included
1/3 cup Onion, minced
1/3 cup Celery, finely chopped
2 Eggs
3 oz. pkg. Cream cheese, reduced or non-fat, softened
1 tsp. Salt
1/2 tsp. Basil, finely chopped fresh or crushed dry
1/4 tsp. Rosemary, finely chopped fresh or crushed dry
1/4 tsp. Oregano, finely chopped fresh or crushed dry
1 1/2 Tbsp. Brandy
Pepper to taste

INSTRUCTIONS:

Melt butter in a pan and briskly cook with mushrooms, onions and celery, 3 to 5 minutes. Beat eggs with cream cheese until well blended; add to mushroom mixture. Stir in brandy, salt, basil, rosemary, oregano and pepper.

Butter a 7"x 4"x 2" loaf pan and line with wax paper, leaving the ends hang over. Fill pan with the mushroom mixture and bake in a preheated 400°F oven 1 1/2 hours or until firm.

Cool to lukewarm before removing from pan, using wax paper ends as an aid. Slice loaf and blend in a food processor or blender until smooth. If some more liquid is needed add more brandy 1 Tbsp at a time during the blending process.

Serve with crackers or thinly sliced toast rounds as an appetizer.

Pairs well with Hatfield Creek Zinfandel

NOTES

Zinfandel Caprese Salad

SIDE DISH

Elevate the classic Caprese salad with a Zinfandel wine twist. This refreshing salad combines ripe tomatoes, fresh mozzarella, and fragrant basil, all drizzled with a Zinfandel-infused balsamic vinaigrette. Makes 4 servings.

Ingredients:

For the Salad:
- 4 large ripe tomatoes, sliced
- 8 ounces fresh mozzarella cheese, sliced
- Fresh basil leaves
- Salt and freshly ground black pepper, to taste

For the Zinfandel-Infused Balsamic Vinaigrette:
- 1/4 cup Zinfandel wine
- 3 tablespoons balsamic vinegar
- 2 tablespoons extra-virgin olive oil
- 1 clove garlic, minced
- 1 teaspoon honey
- Salt and freshly ground black pepper, to taste

INSTRUCTIONS:

1. Prepare the Zinfandel-Infused Balsamic Vinaigrette:
In a small saucepan, combine the Zinfandel wine and balsamic vinegar. Bring the mixture to a gentle simmer over low heat and cook for about 5-7 minutes, or until it's reduced by half. Remove it from heat and let it cool.

2. Make the Vinaigrette:
In a bowl, whisk together the Zinfandel and balsamic reduction, extra-virgin olive oil, minced garlic, honey, salt, and black pepper. Mix until well combined. Set aside.

3. Assemble the Salad:
On a serving platter, arrange the sliced tomatoes and fresh mozzarella cheese. Tuck fresh basil leaves between the tomato and mozzarella slices. Season the salad with a pinch of salt and freshly ground black pepper.

4. Drizzle with Zinfandel-Infused Vinaigrette:
Just before serving, drizzle the Zinfandel-Infused Balsamic Vinaigrette generously over the Caprese salad.

5. Serve:
Serve it as an appetizer or side dish and savor the delightful combination of fresh flavors with a hint of Zinfandel wine.

NOTES

Zinfandel Roasted Brussels Sprouts

SIDE DISH

Elevate your Brussels sprouts to a new level of flavor with a Zinfandel wine glaze. These roasted Brussels sprouts are crispy, caramelized, and drizzled with a sweet and savory Zinfandel reduction, creating a side dish that's both elegant and delicious. Makes 4 servings.

Ingredients:

For the Roasted Brussels Sprouts:
- 1 pound Brussels sprouts, trimmed and halved
- 2 tablespoons olive oil
- Salt and freshly ground black pepper, to taste

For the Zinfandel Glaze:
- 1/2 cup Zinfandel wine
- 2 tablespoons balsamic vinegar
- 2 tablespoons honey
- 1 tablespoon Dijon mustard
- 2 cloves garlic, minced
- Salt and freshly ground black pepper, to taste

Instructions:

1. Preheat the Oven:
Preheat your oven to 400°F (200°C).

2. Roast the Brussels Sprouts:
In a large mixing bowl, toss the halved Brussels sprouts with olive oil, salt, and freshly ground black pepper until they're evenly coated. Spread the Brussels sprouts in a single layer on a baking sheet.

3. Roast in the Oven:
Roast the Brussels sprouts in the preheated oven for about 25-30 minutes, or until they're tender and the edges are crispy and caramelized. Stir them once or twice during roasting for even cooking.

4. Prepare the Zinfandel Glaze:
While the Brussels sprouts are roasting, prepare the Zinfandel glaze. In a small saucepan, combine the Zinfandel wine, balsamic vinegar, honey, Dijon mustard, minced garlic, salt, and black pepper. Bring the mixture to a boil, then reduce the heat and simmer for about 10-15 minutes, or until the glaze thickens to a syrupy consistency.

5. Glaze the Brussels Sprouts:
Once the Brussels sprouts are roasted to perfection, remove them from the oven. Drizzle the Zinfandel glaze over the roasted Brussels sprouts, tossing them gently to ensure they're well coated.

6. Serve:
Transfer to a serving dish and serve immediately. Enjoy this delectable side dish as a complement to your main course.

Notes

Zinfandel Beef Tenderloin

MAIN COURSE

Elevate your dinner with this exquisite dish. Succulent beef tenderloin is seared to perfection and served with a rich mushroom sauce infused with the deep, complex flavors of Zinfandel wine. Makes 4 servings.

Ingredients:

For the Beef Tenderloin:
- 1.5 pounds beef tenderloin, cut into 4 equal steaks
- Salt and freshly ground black pepper, to taste
- 2 tablespoons olive oil
- 2 cloves garlic, minced
- 1 tablespoon fresh rosemary, chopped (or 1 teaspoon dried rosemary)

For the Mushroom Sauce:
- 2 tablespoons unsalted butter
- 1 pound cremini mushrooms, sliced
- 2 shallots, finely chopped
- 1/2 cup Zinfandel wine
- 1 cup beef broth
- 1/2 cup heavy cream
- Salt and freshly ground black pepper, to taste
- Fresh parsley, for garnish (optional)

INSTRUCTIONS:

1. Season the Beef Tenderloin:
Pat the beef tenderloin steaks dry with paper towels. Season both sides generously with salt and freshly ground black pepper.

2. Sear the Beef:
Heat the olive oil in a large skillet over medium-high heat. Add the minced garlic and chopped rosemary. Cook for about 30 seconds until fragrant. Place the beef tenderloin steaks in the skillet and sear for 3-4 minutes on each side for medium-rare, adjusting the cooking time to your preferred level of doneness. Remove the steaks from the skillet and let them rest on a plate, loosely covered with foil.

3. Prepare the Mushroom Sauce:
In the same skillet, add the butter and sliced cremini mushrooms. Sauté the mushrooms for about 5-7 minutes until they become golden brown and release their moisture. Add the finely chopped shallots and continue to cook for another 2-3 minutes until the shallots are translucent.

4. Deglaze with Zinfandel:
Pour in the Zinfandel wine, scraping the browned bits from the bottom of the skillet with a wooden spoon. Simmer for 2-3 minutes to reduce the wine slightly.

5. Create the Mushroom Cream Sauce:
Stir in the beef broth and heavy cream. Bring the mixture to a gentle simmer and cook for 5-7 minutes, allowing the sauce to thicken. Season with salt and freshly ground black pepper to taste.

6. Serve:
Place the seared beef tenderloin steaks on serving plates and spoon the Zinfandel wine-infused mushroom sauce over them. Garnish with fresh parsley if desired.

NOTES

Zinfandel Beef Fajitas

MAIN COURSE

Take your beef fajitas to the next level with a flavorful Zinfandel wine marinade. Tender strips of beef are infused with rich, fruity Zinfandel wine, then grilled to perfection and served with sizzling peppers and onions. Makes 4 servings.

Ingredients:

For the Zinfandel Wine Marinade:
- 1/2 cup Zinfandel wine
- 2 cloves garlic, minced
- 1 teaspoon ground cumin
- 1 teaspoon chili powder
- 1/2 teaspoon paprika
- Salt and freshly ground black pepper, to taste

For the Beef Fajitas:
- 1.5 pounds flank steak, skirt steak, or sirloin, thinly sliced against the grain
- 2 bell peppers, thinly sliced (a mix of colors is great)
- 1 large onion, thinly sliced
- 2 tablespoons olive oil
- 8 small flour tortillas, warmed
- Optional toppings: sour cream, guacamole, salsa, shredded cheese, chopped fresh cilantro, lime wedges

INSTRUCTIONS:

1. Prepare the Zinfandel Wine Marinade:
In a bowl, whisk together the Zinfandel wine, minced garlic, ground cumin, chili powder, paprika, salt, and black pepper.

2. Marinate the Beef:
Place the thinly sliced beef in a large resealable plastic bag or a shallow dish. Pour the Zinfandel wine marinade over the beef and seal the bag or cover the dish. Refrigerate for at least 1 hour, or ideally, overnight, allowing the flavors to meld and the beef to absorb the wine-infused seasonings.

3. Sear the Beef:
Preheat your grill or grill pan to high heat. Remove the beef from the marinade and let any excess liquid drip off. Grill the marinated beef for 2-3 minutes per side or until it reaches your preferred level of doneness. Cooking times may vary depending on the thickness of the beef and your grill's heat. Remove the beef from the grill and let it rest for a few minutes.

4. Sauté the Peppers and Onions:
While the beef is resting, heat the olive oil in a large skillet over medium-high heat. Add the thinly sliced bell peppers and onions to the skillet. Sauté for 5-7 minutes, or until they are tender and slightly caramelized.

5. Assemble the Fajitas:
Warm the flour tortillas in the oven or on the grill for a few seconds. Place a portion of grilled Zinfandel wine-marinated beef on each tortilla. Top with the sautéed peppers and onions.

Serve with your choice of toppings such as sour cream, guacamole, salsa, shredded cheese, chopped fresh cilantro, and lime wedges.

NOTES

Zinfandel Pork Marsala

MAIN COURSE

Elevate your classic Pork Marsala with a twist of Zinfandel wine. Juicy pork medallions and sautéed mushrooms are bathed in a rich and velvety Zinfandel wine sauce, creating a delectable Italian-inspired dish. Makes 4 servings.

Ingredients:

- 4 boneless pork loin chops (about 1 inch thick)
- Salt and black pepper, to taste
- 1/2 cup all-purpose flour, for dredging
- 2 tablespoons olive oil
- 2 tablespoons unsalted butter
- 8 ounces cremini or white mushrooms, sliced
- 1/2 cup Zinfandel wine
- 1/2 cup chicken broth
- 1/4 cup Marsala wine
- 2 cloves garlic, minced
- 2 tablespoons fresh parsley, chopped, for garnish

Instructions:

1. Prepare the Pork:
Season the pork loin chops with salt and black pepper. Dredge each pork chop in the flour, shaking off any excess.

2. Sear the Pork:
In a large skillet, heat the olive oil and 1 tablespoon of butter over medium-high heat. Add the pork chops to the skillet and cook for about 4-5 minutes on each side, or until they are browned and cooked through. Remove the pork chops from the skillet and set them aside.

3. Sauté the Mushrooms:
In the same skillet, add the remaining 1 tablespoon of butter. Add the sliced mushrooms and minced garlic to the skillet. Sauté for about 5-7 minutes, or until the mushrooms are tender and browned.

4. Create the Zinfandel Wine Marsala Sauce:
Pour in the Zinfandel wine, Marsala wine, and chicken broth, stirring to combine. Bring the mixture to a simmer and let it cook for about 10 minutes, or until the sauce has reduced and thickened slightly.

5. Return the Pork and Serve:
Return the seared pork chops to the skillet, allowing them to heat through in the sauce for a few minutes.

6. Garnish and Serve:
Sprinkle the chopped fresh parsley over the top. Serve the pork chops with a generous spoonful of the flavorful Zinfandel wine and Marsala sauce.

Notes

Zinfandel Turkey Enchiladas

MAIN COURSE

These Zinfandel Wine Turkey Enchiladas are a delightful twist on a Mexican classic. Tender turkey and sautéed vegetables are wrapped in corn tortillas, smothered in a rich Zinfandel wine sauce, and baked to cheesy perfection. Makes 4 servings.

Ingredients:

For the Enchiladas:
- 2 cups cooked turkey, shredded
- 1 onion, chopped
- 1 red bell pepper, chopped
- 1 jalapeño pepper, seeded and finely chopped (adjust to your heat preference)
- 2 cloves garlic, minced
- 1 cup black beans, drained and rinsed
- 1 cup corn kernels (fresh, frozen, or canned)
- 8 small corn tortillas
- 2 cups shredded Monterey Jack or Mexican blend cheese
- Salt and black pepper, to taste
- Fresh cilantro, for garnish

For the Zinfandel Wine Sauce:
- 1 cup Zinfandel wine
- 1 cup tomato sauce
- 1 teaspoon chili powder
- 1/2 teaspoon ground cumin
- 1/2 teaspoon dried oregano
- Salt and black pepper, to taste

INSTRUCTIONS:

1. Sauté the Vegetables:
In a large skillet, heat some olive oil over medium heat. Add the chopped onion, red bell pepper, jalapeño pepper, and minced garlic. Sauté for about 5-7 minutes, or until the vegetables are softened.

2. Prepare the Zinfandel Wine Sauce:
Pour in the Zinfandel wine and tomato sauce. Stir in the chili powder, ground cumin, dried oregano, salt, and black pepper. Allow the sauce to simmer for about 10 minutes, or until it has thickened and the flavors meld together. Adjust seasoning if needed.

3. Assemble the Enchiladas:
Preheat your oven to 350°F (175°C). In a large mixing bowl, combine the shredded turkey, sautéed vegetables, black beans, and corn. Mix everything together. Warm the corn tortillas briefly in the microwave or a dry skillet to make them pliable. Spoon some of the turkey mixture onto each tortilla, roll them up, and place them seam-side down in a baking dish.

4. Pour on the Zinfandel Wine Sauce:
Pour the prepared Zinfandel wine sauce evenly over the turkey enchiladas.

5. Bake and Garnish:
Sprinkle the shredded cheese over the top of the enchiladas. Bake in the preheated oven for about 20-25 minutes, or until the enchiladas are heated through and the cheese is bubbly and golden. Garnish with fresh cilantro.

NOTES

Zinfandel
Double-Chocolate Mousse Cake

DESSERT

Indulge in the luxurious decadence of this Zinfandel Wine Double-Chocolate Mousse Cake. Layers of rich chocolate cake are soaked in a Zinfandel wine syrup and alternated with velvety chocolate mousse, creating a dessert that's a true delight for chocolate lovers. Makes 10-12 servings.

Ingredients:

For the Chocolate Cake:
- 1 and 3/4 cups all-purpose flour
- 1 and 3/4 cups granulated sugar
- 3/4 cup unsweetened cocoa powder
- 1 and 1/2 teaspoons baking powder
- 1 and 1/2 teaspoons baking soda
- 1 teaspoon salt
- 2 large eggs
- 1 cup buttermilk
- 1/2 cup vegetable oil
- 2 teaspoons pure vanilla extract
- 1 cup Zinfandel wine

For the Zinfandel Wine Syrup:
- 1/2 cup Zinfandel wine
- 1/4 cup granulated sugar

For the Chocolate Mousse:
- 10 ounces semisweet chocolate, chopped
- 2 cups heavy cream, divided
- 1/4 cup powdered sugar
- 1 teaspoon pure vanilla extract

For Garnish:
- Shaved chocolate or cocoa powder

INSTRUCTIONS:

1. Prepare the Chocolate Cake:
Preheat your oven to 350°F (175°C). Grease and flour two 9-inch round cake pans. In a large mixing bowl, whisk together the flour, sugar, cocoa powder, baking powder, baking soda, and salt. Add the eggs, buttermilk, vegetable oil, and vanilla extract. Mix until the batter is smooth. Gradually pour in the Zinfandel wine and mix until well combined. Divide the batter evenly between the prepared cake pans. Bake for 25-30 minutes or until a toothpick inserted into the center of the cakes comes out clean. Remove the cakes from the oven and let them cool in the pans for 10 minutes. Then, transfer them to a wire rack to cool completely.

2. Make the Zinfandel Wine Syrup:
In a small saucepan, combine the Zinfandel wine and granulated sugar. Bring the mixture to a boil over medium heat, stirring until the sugar has dissolved. Reduce the heat and simmer for about 5 minutes, or until the syrup thickens slightly. Remove it from the heat and let it cool.

3. Prepare the Chocolate Mousse:
Place the chopped semisweet chocolate in a heatproof bowl. In a separate saucepan, heat 1 cup of heavy cream until it's hot but not boiling. Pour the hot cream over the chopped chocolate and let it sit for a minute. Then, stir until the chocolate is completely melted and the mixture is smooth. Allow it to cool to room temperature. In another mixing bowl, whip the remaining
1 cup of heavy cream until it begins to thicken. Add the powdered sugar and vanilla extract to the whipped cream. Continue whipping until stiff peaks form. Gently fold the cooled chocolate mixture into the whipped cream until well combined.

4. Assemble the Mousse Cake:
Place one of the chocolate cake layers on a serving platter. Drizzle half of the Zinfandel wine syrup evenly over the cake layer. Spread a generous layer of chocolate mousse on top of the soaked cake layer. Place the second cake layer on top of the mousse layer. Drizzle the remaining Zinfandel wine syrup evenly over the second cake layer. Cover the entire cake with the remaining chocolate mousse, spreading it smoothly.

5. Chill and Garnish:
Refrigerate the cake for at least 4 hours or until the mousse is set. Before serving, garnish with shaved chocolate or a dusting of cocoa powder for an elegant finish.

Zinfandel Grilled Peaches

DESSERT

Zinfandel Wine Grilled Peaches are a delightful summer dessert. Juicy, ripe peaches are infused with a Zinfandel wine glaze and grilled to perfection, creating a sweet and tangy treat. Makes 4 servings.

Ingredients:

- 4 ripe peaches, halved and pitted
- 1 cup Zinfandel wine
- 1/4 cup honey
- 1 teaspoon vanilla extract
- 1/2 teaspoon ground cinnamon
- Vanilla ice cream (optional, for serving)
- Fresh mint leaves, for garnish

Instructions:

1. Prepare the Zinfandel Wine Glaze:
In a small saucepan, combine the Zinfandel wine, honey, vanilla extract, and ground cinnamon. Bring the mixture to a boil over medium-high heat, stirring occasionally. Reduce the heat to low and simmer for about 10-15 minutes, or until the glaze thickens and reduces by half. Remove it from the heat and let it cool to room temperature.

2. Preheat the Grill:
Preheat your grill to medium-high heat. Make sure the grates are clean and lightly oiled to prevent sticking.

3. Grill the Peaches:
Brush the cut sides of the peach halves with a little of the Zinfandel wine glaze. Place the peaches, cut side down, on the grill grates. Grill for about 2-3 minutes, or until grill marks appear and the peaches are slightly softened.

4. Glaze the Peaches:
Carefully flip the peaches over using tongs. Brush the tops of the peaches with more of the Zinfandel wine glaze. Continue grilling for another 2-3 minutes, allowing the peaches to caramelize and absorb the flavors of the glaze.

5. Serve:
Remove the grilled peaches from the grill and place them on a serving platter. Drizzle any remaining Zinfandel wine glaze over the peaches. Serve warm, either on their own or with a scoop of vanilla ice cream for an extra indulgence.

Garnish with fresh mint leaves for a pop of color and freshness.

Notes

SANGIOVESE
Wine Notes

~ Food Pairing Suggestions ~

Italian Cuisine: Sangiovese is a natural partner for classic Italian dishes such as pasta with tomato-based sauces, pizza, lasagna, and risotto.

Red Meat: Its acidity and moderate tannins make it a versatile choice for red meat dishes like roast lamb, grilled steak, and hearty stews.

Mushroom Dishes: Sangiovese's earthy notes harmonize beautifully with mushroom-based dishes, like mushroom risotto or a mushroom and goat cheese tart.

Hard Cheeses: Pair it with aged cheeses like pecorino or Parmesan.

Poultry: It complements poultry dishes, particularly those with tomato-based or herb-infused sauces.

Charcuterie: Enjoy Sangiovese with a charcuterie board featuring cured meats and a variety of cheeses.

Herb-Seasoned Dishes: Sangiovese's herbal undertones pair well with dishes seasoned with fresh herbs, such as rosemary or thyme.

Vegetarian Dishes: It complements vegetarian dishes like eggplant Parmesan or grilled portobello mushrooms.

Tomato-Based Appetizers: Its acidity pairs nicely with tomato-based appetizers, like bruschetta or caprese salad.

PRIMARY FLAVORS
~

Red Fruit Notes: Predominantly red fruit flavors like cherry, strawberry, and raspberry, often with a tart or tangy edge.

Floral and Herbal Notes: Sangiovese can feature floral notes like violet and herbal hints such as thyme and oregano.

Earthiness: Some Sangiovese wines showcase earthy characteristics like dried leaves or a subtle tobacco note.

Oak Influence: Depending on aging, you may detect notes of vanilla, spice, or toast.

TASTE PROFILE
~

Body: Typically medium-bodied, but this can vary based on the region and winemaking style.

Acidity: Sangiovese is known for its high acidity, which provides brightness and structure.

Tannins: Generally moderate to high, giving the wine a firm structure.

Alcohol: Often moderate, but it can vary depending on the region and climate.

Finish: Crisp and refreshing with a medium to long finish.

Chapter Five
Sangiovese

Step into the world of Sangiovese, a wine that whispers tales of sun-drenched Italian landscapes and holds within its ruby depths a vibrant legacy of flavors. Sangiovese is not just a wine; it's a symphony of tastes and aromas that beckon you to explore its culinary potential.

In this chapter, we invite you to embark on a journey that celebrates Sangiovese's distinctive qualities, both in the glass and in the pot. Beyond its reputation as a bright and lively wine, Sangiovese reveals an innate ability to elevate the flavors of countless dishes, creating culinary magic with every sip.

Sangiovese's signature characteristics, including tart red fruit notes, herbal hints, and a refreshing acidity, make it a versatile canvas upon which to craft a culinary masterpiece. Whether you're preparing a classic Italian pasta dish, indulging in a hearty stew, or savoring the flavors of a Mediterranean feast, Sangiovese is the perfect partner.

Join us as we explore Sangiovese's flavor profile, marked by bright cherry and raspberry notes, a touch of earthiness, and an herbal bouquet. Through the recipes and techniques in this chapter, you'll discover how to harness the potential of Sangiovese, creating dishes that sing with harmony and zest.

Sangiovese Brandy Bliss
COCKTAIL

The Sangiovese Brandy Bliss is a harmonious and sophisticated cocktail that marries the rich warmth of brandy with the robust character of Sangiovese wine. It's a blissful fusion of flavors that's perfect for sipping and savoring. Makes one cocktail, easily scalable for multiple servings.

Ingredients:

- 1 1/2 oz Sangiovese wine
- 1 1/2 oz brandy
- 1/2 oz simple syrup (adjust to taste)
- 1 dash orange bitters
- Ice cubes
- Orange twist or cherry for garnish (optional)

INSTRUCTIONS:

1. Chill Your Glass:
Place a brandy snifter or rocks glass in the freezer to chill.

2. Prepare the Cocktail:
In a mixing glass filled with ice, combine the Sangiovese wine, brandy, simple syrup, and orange bitters.

3. Stir Well:
Stir the mixture gently for about 15-20 seconds. This chills the ingredients and properly dilutes the drink.

4. Strain and Serve:
Remove the chilled glass from the freezer and strain the cocktail into it.

5. Garnish:
If desired, garnish your Sangiovese Brandy Bliss with an orange twist or a maraschino cherry.

6. Enjoy:
Sip and savor this blissful cocktail that combines the richness of brandy with the deep character of Sangiovese wine. It's an ideal choice for a cozy evening by the fire or as an after-dinner treat.

NOTES

Sangiovese
Cherry Whiskey Sour

COCKTAIL

Savor the delightful fusion of Sangiovese wine, whiskey, and juicy cherries in this captivating cocktail. It's a perfect harmony of rich, fruity flavors with a hint of whiskey's warmth. Makes one cocktail.

Ingredients:

- 2 oz Sangiovese wine
- 1 1/2 oz whiskey
- 1 oz freshly squeezed lemon juice
- 1/2 oz cherry liqueur
- 1/2 oz simple syrup
- Ice
- Maraschino cherry and lemon slice (for garnish)

INSTRUCTIONS:

1. In a cocktail shaker, combine Sangiovese wine, whiskey, freshly squeezed lemon juice, cherry liqueur, and simple syrup.

2. Fill the shaker with ice and shake vigorously for about 15 seconds until well chilled.

3. Strain the mixture into a rocks glass filled with ice.

4. Garnish with a maraschino cherry and a slice of lemon.

5. Take a sip and let the sweet cherry notes dance with the robust Sangiovese and the boldness of whiskey. Enjoy your Sangiovese Cherry Whiskey Sour!

NOTES

Sangiovese

Cucumber-Stuffed Cherry Tomatoes

APPETIZER

Sangiovese Wine Cucumber-Stuffed Cherry Tomatoes are a delightful appetizer that combines the juicy sweetness of cherry tomatoes with the crisp freshness of cucumbers, all enhanced by the rich notes of Sangiovese wine. These bite-sized treats are perfect for elegant gatherings or as a refreshing snack. Makes 4-6 servings.

Ingredients:

- 24 cherry tomatoes
- 1 cucumber, finely diced
- 1/4 cup Sangiovese wine
- 2 tablespoons red onion, finely minced
- 2 tablespoons fresh basil, chopped
- 2 tablespoons extra-virgin olive oil
- 1 clove garlic, minced
- Salt and black pepper to taste
- Fresh basil leaves for garnish

INSTRUCTIONS:

1. Prepare the Cherry Tomatoes:
Cut the tops off the cherry tomatoes and carefully hollow them out using a small spoon. Place the hollowed tomatoes upside down on paper towels to drain excess moisture.

2. Prepare the Filling:
In a mixing bowl, combine the finely diced cucumber, Sangiovese wine, minced red onion, chopped fresh basil, extra-virgin olive oil, minced garlic, salt, and black pepper. Mix well to combine.

3. Marinate:
Allow the cucumber mixture to marinate in the Sangiovese wine for about 15-20 minutes. This will infuse the flavors of the wine into the cucumber.

4. Fill the Tomatoes:
Gently pat the hollowed cherry tomatoes dry with a paper towel. Fill each tomato with a small spoonful of the marinated cucumber mixture.

5. Chill:
Place the stuffed cherry tomatoes in the refrigerator for at least 30 minutes to allow the flavors to meld and the tomatoes to chill.

6. Garnish and Serve:
Before serving, garnish with fresh basil leaves. Arrange them on a serving platter and enjoy!

NOTES

Sangiovese Bourbon Ham Balls

APPETIZER

These Bourbon Ham Balls are the ultimate combination of sweet, savory, and a touch of sophistication. Featuring a luscious Sangiovese wine glaze, they're the perfect appetizer or main course for your next gathering. Makes about 20 ham balls.

Ingredients:

For the Ham Balls:
- 1 1/2 pounds ground ham
- 1 1/2 pounds ground pork
- 1 cup breadcrumbs
- 1/2 cup milk
- 1/2 cup finely minced onion
- 2 large eggs, beaten
- 1/4 cup brown sugar
- 1/4 cup bourbon
- 1/4 teaspoon ground cloves
- 1/4 teaspoon ground nutmeg
- Salt and black pepper to taste

For the Sangiovese Glaze:
- 1 1/2 cups Sangiovese wine
- 1/2 cup brown sugar
- 1/4 cup ketchup
- 1/4 cup apple cider vinegar
- 1/4 cup water
- 1/4 cup soy sauce
- 2 cloves garlic, minced
- 1 teaspoon ginger, grated
- 1/2 teaspoon red pepper flakes (adjust to taste)

INSTRUCTIONS:

1. Preheat the Oven:
Preheat your oven to 350°F (175°C).

2. Prepare the Ham Ball Mixture:
In a large mixing bowl, combine the ground ham, ground pork, breadcrumbs, milk, minced onion, eggs, brown sugar, bourbon, ground cloves, ground nutmeg, salt, and black pepper. Mix until all ingredients are well combined.

3. Shape the Ham Balls:
Roll the mixture into 1 to 1.5-inch meatballs and arrange them on a baking sheet lined with parchment paper.

4. Bake the Ham Balls:
Bake in the preheated oven for 30-35 minutes or until the ham balls are cooked through and golden brown.

5. Prepare the Sangiovese Glaze:
While the ham balls are baking, make the Sangiovese glaze. In a saucepan, combine the Sangiovese wine, brown sugar, ketchup, apple cider vinegar, water, soy sauce, minced garlic, grated ginger, and red pepper flakes. Bring to a simmer and cook for about 15-20 minutes, or until the glaze thickens.

6. Glaze the Ham Balls:
Once the ham balls are done, remove them from the oven and brush generously with the Sangiovese glaze. Return them to the oven for an additional 5-10 minutes, allowing the glaze to caramelize and create a deliciously sticky coating.

7. Serve:
Serve as an appetizer or as a main course with your favorite side dishes. Garnish with fresh herbs if desired.

NOTES

Sangiovese
Turkey and Mushroom Risotto

SIDE DISH

Sangiovese Wine Turkey and Mushroom Risotto is a hearty and flavorful dish. Creamy Arborio rice is cooked with tender turkey, earthy mushrooms, and infused with the rich, robust notes of Sangiovese wine, creating a comforting Italian-inspired meal. Makes 4 servings.

Ingredients:

- 1 cup Arborio rice
- 1/2 pound turkey breast, diced into small pieces
- 8 oz mushrooms (cremini or shiitake), sliced
- 1 small onion, finely chopped
- 2 cloves garlic, minced
- 1/2 cup Sangiovese wine
- 4 cups chicken or vegetable broth, kept warm
- 2 tablespoons olive oil
- 2 tablespoons butter
- 1/2 cup grated Parmesan cheese
- Salt and black pepper to taste
- Fresh parsley, chopped (for garnish)

INSTRUCTIONS:

NOTES

1. Sauté Turkey and Mushrooms:
In a large skillet or saucepan, heat the olive oil over medium-high heat. Add the diced turkey pieces and cook until they are browned and cooked through, about 5-7 minutes. Remove them from the skillet and set them aside. In the same skillet, add the sliced mushrooms and cook until they are browned and any liquid has evaporated, about 5-7 minutes. Remove them from the skillet and set them aside.

2. Cook Onions and Garlic:
In the same skillet, add the chopped onions and garlic. Sauté until the onions become translucent, about 3-4 minutes.

3. Toast Rice:
Add the Arborio rice to the skillet and stir to coat it with the onion and garlic mixture. Toast the rice for 1-2 minutes until it becomes slightly translucent around the edges.

4. Deglaze with Wine:
Pour in the Sangiovese wine and cook, stirring constantly, until the wine is mostly absorbed by the rice.

5. Start Adding Broth:
Begin adding the warm broth, one ladle at a time, stirring continuously and allowing the liquid to be absorbed before adding more. Continue this process until the rice is creamy and cooked to your desired level of doneness. This usually takes about 18-20 minutes.

6. Add Turkey and Mushrooms:
About halfway through cooking the rice, return the cooked turkey and mushrooms to the skillet. Stir them into the rice.

7. Finish the Risotto:
Once the rice is cooked and creamy, remove the skillet from heat. Stir in the butter and grated Parmesan cheese until they are melted and the risotto is creamy. Season with salt and black pepper to taste.

8. Serve:
Spoon onto plates or into bowls. Garnish with chopped fresh parsley for a pop of color and freshness. Serve hot and enjoy!

Sangiovese

Mexican Zucchini Boats

SIDE DISH

Sangiovese Wine Mexican Zucchini Boats are a delightful fusion of flavors. Zucchini halves are filled with a savory mixture of ground beef, beans, corn, and tomatoes, then baked to perfection and drizzled with a Sangiovese wine-infused sauce for a delicious twist on a classic dish. Makes 4 servings.

Ingredients:

For the Zucchini Boats:
- 2 large zucchini
- 1/2 pound ground beef
- 1/2 cup black beans, cooked and drained
- 1/2 cup corn kernels (fresh, frozen, or canned)
- 1/2 cup diced tomatoes
- 1/2 cup diced red bell pepper
- 1/2 cup diced onion
- 2 cloves garlic, minced
- 1 teaspoon chili powder
- 1/2 teaspoon ground cumin
- Salt and black pepper to taste
- 1 cup shredded cheddar cheese (or your favorite cheese)

For the Sangiovese Wine Sauce:
- 1/2 cup Sangiovese wine
- 1/4 cup tomato sauce
- 1 tablespoon olive oil
- 1/2 teaspoon dried oregano
- Salt and black pepper to taste

INSTRUCTIONS:

1. Prepare the Zucchini:
Preheat your oven to 375°F (190°C). Slice the zucchini in half lengthwise. Use a spoon to carefully scoop out the center flesh, leaving a zucchini "boat" with about 1/4-inch thickness.

2. Prepare the Filling:
In a large skillet, heat olive oil over medium-high heat. Add the diced onion and red bell pepper. Sauté until they begin to soften, about 3-4 minutes. Add the minced garlic and cook for an additional 1 minute until fragrant. Add the ground beef and cook until browned and crumbled, breaking it up with a spoon as it cooks. Stir in the chili powder, ground cumin, salt, and black pepper. Add the diced tomatoes, black beans, and corn. Cook for another 2-3 minutes until the mixture is heated through.

3. Fill the Zucchini Boats:
Place the zucchini boats in a baking dish. Spoon the beef and vegetable mixture evenly into the zucchini boats.

4. Prepare the Sangiovese Wine Sauce:
In a small saucepan, combine the Sangiovese wine, tomato sauce, dried oregano, salt, and black pepper. Bring the sauce to a simmer over medium heat and cook for 5-7 minutes until it thickens slightly.

5. Bake the Zucchini Boats:
Pour the Sangiovese wine sauce over the filled zucchini boats. Cover the baking dish with aluminum foil and bake in the preheated oven for 25-30 minutes or until the zucchini is tender.

6. Add Cheese and Finish:
Remove the foil and sprinkle shredded cheddar cheese over the zucchini boats. Return the dish to the oven and bake, uncovered, for an additional 5-7 minutes, or until the cheese is melted and bubbly.

7. Serve:
Carefully transfer to serving plates. Drizzle any remaining sauce from the baking dish over the top. Serve hot and enjoy your flavorful zucchini boat creation!

NOTES

Sangiovese
Sesame Beef Skewers
MAIN COURSE

Sangiovese Wine Sesame Beef Skewers are a delightful fusion of savory and slightly sweet flavors. Tender beef strips are marinated in a Sangiovese wine mixture, then skewered and grilled to perfection, all while being brushed with a delicious sesame glaze. Makes 2 servings.

Ingredients:

For the Beef Marinade:
- 1 pound beef sirloin or flank steak, thinly sliced into strips
- 1/2 cup Sangiovese wine
- 2 cloves garlic, minced
- 2 tablespoons soy sauce
- 1 tablespoon honey
- 1 tablespoon sesame oil
- 1/2 teaspoon ground ginger
- Salt and black pepper to taste

For the Sesame Glaze:
- 2 tablespoons honey
- 1 tablespoon sesame seeds
- 1 tablespoon soy sauce
- 1 tablespoon rice vinegar
- 1/2 teaspoon sesame oil

For Skewering:
- Wooden skewers, soaked in water for at least 30 minutes (to prevent burning)

Instructions:

1. Prepare the Beef Marinade:
In a mixing bowl, combine Sangiovese wine, minced garlic, soy sauce, honey, sesame oil, ground ginger, salt, and black pepper. Add the thinly sliced beef strips to the marinade. Toss to coat evenly. Cover the bowl and let the beef marinate in the refrigerator for at least 30 minutes, or up to 2 hours for maximum flavor.

2. Prepare the Sesame Glaze:
In a small saucepan over low heat, combine honey, sesame seeds, soy sauce, rice vinegar, and sesame oil. Stir and heat the mixture until the honey is fully dissolved and the glaze thickens slightly, about 3-4 minutes. Remove from heat.

3. Skewer the Beef:
Preheat your grill to medium-high heat. Thread the marinated beef strips onto the soaked wooden skewers, keeping them flat and evenly spaced.

4. Grill the Skewers:
Place the skewers on the preheated grill. Grill for about 2-3 minutes per side, or until the beef is cooked to your desired level of doneness.

5. Glaze the Skewers:
During the last minute of grilling, brush generously with the sesame glaze on both sides, allowing it to caramelize slightly.

6. Serve:
Carefully remove the skewers from the grill. Transfer the skewers to a serving platter. Serve hot as a delectable appetizer or alongside your favorite side dishes for a main course.

Notes

Sangiovese Pork Ragù

MAIN COURSE

Sangiovese Pork Ragù Over Creamy Polenta is a hearty and comforting Italian-inspired dish. Succulent pork is slow-cooked in Sangiovese wine, tomatoes, and herbs, then served over creamy, cheesy polenta for a truly satisfying meal. Makes 4 servings.

Ingredients:

For the Pork Ragù:
- 1 pound pork shoulder or pork butt, diced into small pieces
- 1 onion, finely chopped
- 2 cloves garlic, minced
- 1 carrot, finely chopped
- 1 celery stalk, finely chopped
- 1/2 cup Sangiovese wine
- 1 can (14 ounces) crushed tomatoes
- 2 tablespoons tomato paste
- 1 teaspoon dried oregano
- 1 teaspoon dried basil
- Salt and black pepper to taste
- 2 tablespoons olive oil
- Fresh basil leaves for garnish (optional)

For the Creamy Polenta:
- 1 cup polenta (cornmeal)
- 4 cups water
- 1 cup milk
- 1/2 cup grated Parmesan cheese
- Salt and black pepper to taste

INSTRUCTIONS:

Prepare the Pork Ragù:

1. In a large, heavy-bottomed pot or Dutch oven, heat olive oil over medium-high heat. Add the diced pork pieces and brown them on all sides. Remove the pork and set it aside.

2. In the same pot, add the chopped onion, garlic, carrot, and celery. Sauté for about 5 minutes, or until the vegetables are softened.

3. Return the browned pork to the pot. Pour in the Sangiovese wine, crushed tomatoes, tomato paste, dried oregano, dried basil, salt, and black pepper. Stir well to combine.

4. Reduce the heat to low, cover the pot, and let the ragù simmer for about 1.5 to 2 hours, or until the pork is tender and the flavors have melded together. Stir occasionally.

Prepare the Creamy Polenta:

1. In a separate saucepan, bring water and milk to a boil. Gradually whisk in the polenta, stirring constantly to avoid lumps.

2. Reduce the heat to low and continue to cook the polenta, stirring often, for about 20-25 minutes or until it becomes thick and creamy.

3. Remove the polenta from heat and stir in the grated Parmesan cheese. Season with salt and black pepper to taste.

Serve:

1. To serve, spoon a generous portion of creamy polenta onto each plate. Top with Ragù. Garnish with fresh basil leaves if desired.

NOTES

Sangiovese Eggplant Parmesan

MAIN COURSE

Sangiovese Eggplant Parmesan is a classic Italian comfort dish with a delightful twist. Layers of crispy breaded eggplant slices are smothered in Sangiovese-infused marinara sauce, topped with melted mozzarella and Parmesan cheese, then baked to perfection. Makes 4 servings.

Ingredients:

For the Eggplant:
- 2 large eggplants, sliced into 1/2-inch rounds
- Salt
- 2 cups all-purpose flour, for dredging
- 3 large eggs
- 2 cups breadcrumbs
- 1 cup grated Parmesan cheese
- Vegetable oil, for frying

For the Sangiovese Marinara Sauce:
- 2 tablespoons olive oil
- 1 onion, finely chopped
- 3 cloves garlic, minced
- 1 (28-ounce) can crushed tomatoes
- 1/2 cup Sangiovese wine
- 2 teaspoons dried basil
- 1 teaspoon dried oregano
- Salt and black pepper to taste

For Assembling:
- 2 cups shredded mozzarella cheese
- 1/2 cup grated Parmesan cheese
- Fresh basil leaves for garnish (optional)

INSTRUCTIONS:

Prepare the Eggplant:

1. Place the eggplant slices on a baking sheet and sprinkle both sides with salt. Let them sit for about 30 minutes to draw out excess moisture. Rinse and pat dry with paper towels.
2. Set up a breading station with three shallow bowls. Place flour in the first bowl, beaten eggs in the second, and a mixture of breadcrumbs and grated Parmesan cheese in the third.
3. Dredge each eggplant slice in flour, then dip into the beaten eggs, and finally coat with the breadcrumb mixture, pressing the breadcrumbs onto the eggplant to adhere.
4. In a large skillet, heat vegetable oil over medium-high heat. Fry the breaded eggplant slices in batches until golden brown on both sides. Place them on paper towels to drain excess oil.

Prepare the Sangiovese Marinara Sauce:

1. In a saucepan, heat olive oil over medium heat. Add chopped onion and sauté until translucent.
2. Stir in minced garlic and sauté for another minute until fragrant.
3. Pour in Sangiovese wine and let it simmer for a few minutes to reduce.
4. Add crushed tomatoes, dried basil, dried oregano, salt, and black pepper. Simmer the sauce for about 15-20 minutes, stirring occasionally.

Assemble and Bake:

1. Preheat your oven to 375°F (190°C).
2. Spread a thin layer of Sangiovese Marinara Sauce on the bottom of a baking dish.
3. Arrange a layer of fried eggplant slices on top of the sauce.
4. Spoon more sauce over the eggplant, then sprinkle with shredded mozzarella and grated Parmesan cheese.
5. Repeat the layering process until you've used all the eggplant, finishing with a layer of sauce and cheese on top.
6. Bake in the preheated oven for 25-30 minutes, or until the cheese is bubbly and golden.
7. Garnish with fresh basil leaves if desired.

Sangiovese Spinach Lasagna

MAIN COURSE

Sangiovese Spinach Lasagna with Ricotta is a rich and flavorful twist on the classic Italian dish. Layers of lasagna noodles, creamy ricotta and spinach filling, Sangiovese-infused marinara sauce, and melted mozzarella come together to create a comforting and indulgent meal. Makes 6-8 servings.

Ingredients:

For the Sangiovese Marinara Sauce:
- 2 tablespoons olive oil
- 1 onion, finely chopped
- 3 cloves garlic, minced
- 1 (28-ounce) can crushed tomatoes
- 1/2 cup Sangiovese wine
- 2 teaspoons dried basil
- 1 teaspoon dried oregano
- Salt and black pepper to taste

For the Ricotta and Spinach Filling:
- 15 ounces ricotta cheese
- 1 egg
- 2 cups fresh spinach, chopped
- 1/2 cup grated Parmesan cheese
- Salt and black pepper to taste

For Assembling:
- 12 lasagna noodles, cooked according to package instructions
- 2 cups shredded mozzarella cheese

INSTRUCTIONS:

Prepare the Sangiovese Marinara Sauce:

1. In a saucepan, heat olive oil over medium heat. Add chopped onion and sauté until translucent.
2. Stir in minced garlic and sauté for another minute until fragrant.
3. Pour in Sangiovese wine and let it simmer for a few minutes to reduce.
4. Add crushed tomatoes, dried basil, dried oregano, salt, and black pepper. Simmer the sauce for about 15-20 minutes, stirring occasionally.

Prepare the Ricotta and Spinach Filling:

1. In a mixing bowl, combine ricotta cheese, one egg, chopped fresh spinach, grated Parmesan cheese, salt, and black pepper. Mix until well combined.

Assemble the Lasagna:

1. Preheat your oven to 375°F (190°C).
2. Spread a thin layer of Sangiovese Marinara Sauce on the bottom of a 9x13-inch baking dish.
3. Place a layer of cooked lasagna noodles over the sauce.
4. Spread half of the ricotta and spinach filling over the noodles.
5. Add another layer of lasagna noodles and top with half of the shredded mozzarella cheese.
6. Repeat the process with another layer of sauce, noodles, ricotta and spinach filling, and mozzarella cheese.
7. Finish with a final layer of lasagna noodles, remaining sauce, and the rest of the mozzarella cheese.
8. Cover the baking dish with aluminum foil.

Bake and Serve:

1. Bake the lasagna in the preheated oven for 30 minutes covered with foil. Then, remove the foil and bake for an additional 15-20 minutes until the top is golden and bubbly.
2. Allow the lasagna to cool for a few minutes before slicing and serving.

NOTES

Sangiovese Tiramisù

DESSERT

Sangiovese Wine Tiramisù is a delightful twist on the classic Italian dessert. This recipe infuses the rich flavors of Sangiovese wine into layers of coffee-soaked ladyfingers and mascarpone cream, creating a heavenly dessert with a hint of sophistication. Makes 6-8 servings.

Ingredients:

- 1 cup Sangiovese wine
- 1/2 cup brewed espresso or strong coffee, cooled
- 24-30 ladyfinger cookies (Savoiardi)
- 1 1/2 cups mascarpone cheese
- 3/4 cup granulated sugar
- 4 large eggs, separated
- 1 teaspoon pure vanilla extract
- Cocoa powder, for dusting
- Dark chocolate shavings, for garnish (optional)

Instructions:

Prepare the Sangiovese Coffee Mixture:

1. In a shallow dish, combine the Sangiovese wine and cooled brewed espresso or coffee.

Prepare the Mascarpone Cream:

1. In a large mixing bowl, whisk together the mascarpone cheese, granulated sugar, egg yolks, and vanilla extract until smooth and well combined.
2. In a separate clean mixing bowl, use an electric mixer to whip the egg whites until stiff peaks form.
3. Gently fold the whipped egg whites into the mascarpone mixture until fully incorporated. Be gentle to maintain the light and airy texture.

Assemble the Sangiovese Wine Tiramisù:

1. Quickly dip each ladyfinger into the Sangiovese coffee mixture, ensuring they are soaked but not overly soggy. Arrange a layer of soaked ladyfingers in the bottom of a serving dish.
2. Spread half of the mascarpone cream mixture over the ladyfingers.
3. Add another layer of soaked ladyfingers on top of the mascarpone layer.
4. Finish with the remaining mascarpone cream, spreading it evenly.

Chill and Serve:

1. Cover the tiramisù with plastic wrap and refrigerate for at least 4 hours, or preferably overnight, to allow the flavors to meld and the dessert to set.
2. Before serving, dust the top with cocoa powder and garnish with dark chocolate shavings, if desired.
3. Serve chilled, and enjoy as a delightful and sophisticated dessert that combines the best of Italian flavors with a wine country twist.

Notes

Sangiovese Cannoli

DESSERT

Sangiovese Wine-Infused Cannoli is a delightful twist on the classic Italian pastry. These crunchy cannoli shells are filled with a luscious mascarpone and Sangiovese wine cream, creating a dessert that's a harmonious blend of rich wine and sweet indulgence. Makes 12-15 cannoli.

Ingredients:

For the Cannoli Shells:
- 1 cup all-purpose flour
- 2 tablespoons granulated sugar
- 1/4 teaspoon salt
- 2 tablespoons unsalted butter, cubed
- 1/4 cup Sangiovese wine
- 1 egg white, lightly beaten
- Vegetable oil, for frying

For the Sangiovese Wine Cannoli Cream:
- 1 1/2 cups mascarpone cheese
- 1/2 cup Sangiovese wine
- 1/2 cup powdered sugar
- 1 teaspoon vanilla extract
- 1/4 cup chopped dark chocolate
- 1/4 cup chopped pistachios (optional)
- Powdered sugar, for dusting

INSTRUCTIONS:

Prepare the Cannoli Shells:

1. In a mixing bowl, combine the flour, granulated sugar, and salt. Add the cubed butter and work it into the dry ingredients until the mixture resembles coarse crumbs.

2. Gradually add the Sangiovese wine and mix until the dough comes together. Knead the dough on a lightly floured surface until it's smooth and elastic, about 5 minutes.

3. Wrap the dough in plastic wrap and let it rest at room temperature for at least 30 minutes.

4. Roll out the dough on a floured surface to about 1/8 inch thickness. Use a round cutter or glass to cut out circles (approximately 4-5 inches in diameter).

5. Wrap each dough circle around a cannoli mold, sealing the edge with the egg white. Ensure the seal is tight to prevent the shells from opening during frying.

6. Heat vegetable oil in a deep, heavy-bottomed pot to 350°F (175°C). Fry the cannoli shells, a few at a time, until golden brown and crispy, about 2-3 minutes. Use tongs to carefully remove them from the oil and drain on paper towels. Let them cool completely before filling.

Prepare the Sangiovese Wine Cannoli Cream:

1. In a mixing bowl, combine the mascarpone cheese, Sangiovese wine, powdered sugar, and vanilla extract. Mix until smooth and well combined.
2. Stir in the chopped dark chocolate and chopped pistachios, if using.

Fill the Cannoli Shells:

1. Just before serving, use a piping bag or a spoon to fill each cooled cannoli shell with the Sangiovese wine cannoli cream. Fill both ends to ensure a creamy center.
2. Dust the filled cannoli with powdered sugar.
3. Serve immediately, and enjoy !

NOTES

SYRAH
Wine Notes

~ Food Pairing Suggestions ~

Red Meat: Syrah's bold flavors and tannic structure make it an ideal companion for red meat dishes like grilled steak, lamb chops, or venison.

Barbecue: It shines with smoky and spicy barbecue dishes, such as pulled pork or smoked brisket.

Game Meats: Syrah pairs beautifully with game meats like duck, wild boar, or quail.

Hard Cheeses: Try it with aged cheeses like cheddar, gouda, or blue cheese.

Grilled Vegetables: Its smoky and peppery notes complement grilled vegetables, especially those with a charred finish.

Spiced Dishes: Syrah's spice characteristics make it a great match for dishes with bold spices, like Moroccan tagines or Indian curries.

Roasted Dishes: It pairs well with roasted dishes, including rosemary-infused roast chicken or herb-crusted pork.

Mushroom-Based Dishes: The earthy qualities in Syrah complement mushroom-based dishes, such as mushroom risotto or a hearty mushroom and truffle pasta.

Chocolate Desserts: Its dark fruit and spice notes harmonize with dark chocolate desserts, like flourless chocolate cake or chocolate mousse.

PRIMARY FLAVORS
~

Dark Fruits:
Syrah is known for its rich, dark fruit flavors such as blackberry, black cherry, and plum.

Spices:
It often features notes of black pepper, cloves, and sometimes more exotic spices like anise.

Earthy Undertones:
Some Syrah wines exhibit earthy qualities, with hints of leather, tobacco, or even game.

Herbal Hints:
Depending on the region and winemaking style, you may detect notes of herbs like thyme or rosemary.

TASTE PROFILE
~

Body:
Generally full-bodied, offering a lush and velvety mouthfeel.

Acidity:
Moderate, providing balance and structure.

Tannins:
Syrah typically has firm to grippy tannins, which contribute to its structure and aging potential.

Alcohol:
Often moderate to high, adding warmth to the wine's profile.

Finish:
Syrah often boasts a long and complex finish, with lingering flavors of dark fruits and spices.

Chapter Six
Syrah

Prepare to immerse yourself in the tantalizing world of Syrah, a wine that beckons with a sultry blend of dark fruits, spices, and a hint of mystery. Syrah is not merely a wine; it's a culinary journey waiting to unfold, and this chapter is your passport to its rich and robust flavors.

In this chapter, we invite you to explore the captivating qualities of Syrah, known for its opulent flavors of blackberries, plums, and an enticing tapestry of spices. Beyond its reputation as a bold and complex wine, Syrah reveals its remarkable prowess as an essential ingredient in elevating your culinary creations.

Syrah's multifaceted flavor profile, characterized by its dark fruit nuances, peppery overtones, and a touch of earthiness, makes it the ideal partner for a myriad of dishes. Whether you're savoring a succulent grilled steak, indulging in hearty game meats, or seeking comfort in a luscious chocolate dessert, Syrah stands ready to enhance your culinary adventures.

Join us as we delve into Syrah's alluring qualities through recipes and techniques that celebrate its culinary magic. Throughout these pages, you'll uncover how to harness the wine's bold and velvety character, transforming your kitchen into a realm of flavors and aromas that dance in harmony.

Syrah Gin Symphony
COCKTAIL

The Syrah Gin Symphony is a captivating and harmonious cocktail that brings together the rich depth of Syrah wine with the botanical elegance of gin. It's a symphony of flavors that's perfect for those who appreciate a balanced and sophisticated drink. Makes one cocktail, easily scalable for multiple servings.

Ingredients:

- 1 1/2 oz Syrah wine
- 1 1/2 oz gin
- 1/2 oz simple syrup (adjust to taste)
- 1 dash orange bitters
- Ice cubes
- Orange twist or blackberry for garnish (optional)

INSTRUCTIONS:

1. Chill Your Glass:
Place a stemmed wine glass or coupe glass in the freezer to chill.

2. Prepare the Cocktail:
In a mixing glass filled with ice, combine the Syrah wine, gin, simple syrup, and orange bitters.

3. Stir Well:
Stir the mixture gently for about 15-20 seconds. This chills the ingredients and ensures proper blending.

4. Strain and Serve:
Remove the chilled glass from the freezer and strain the cocktail into it.

5. Garnish:
If desired, garnish your Syrah Gin Symphony with an orange twist or a blackberry.

6. Enjoy:
Sip and savor this symphony of flavors that combines the robust character of Syrah wine with the botanical charm of gin. It's a versatile and sophisticated choice for cocktail enthusiasts.

NOTES

Syrah Aperol Spritz
COCKTAIL

The Syrah Wine Aperol Spritz is a delightful variation of the classic Italian cocktail. With the bold and robust flavors of Syrah wine, this spritz is a perfect balance of bitterness and sweetness. Ideal for 1 serving.

Ingredients:

- 2 oz Syrah wine
- 1 oz Aperol
- 1 oz club soda
- 1/2 oz fresh orange juice
- Orange slice and a green olive for garnish
- Ice cubes

INSTRUCTIONS:

1. Fill a Glass:
Fill a wine glass or a large goblet with ice cubes.

2. Pour Syrah Wine:
Pour in the Syrah wine over the ice.

3. Add Aperol:
Slowly pour the Aperol over the Syrah wine.

4. Add Fresh Orange Juice:
Pour in the fresh orange juice.

5. Top with Club Soda:
Top off the glass with club soda, and give it a gentle stir to mix the ingredients.

6. Garnish:
Garnish your Syrah Wine Aperol Spritz with a slice of orange and a green olive.

7. Serve:
Serve immediately and enjoy the bold and bittersweet flavors of this delightful cocktail. It's the perfect aperitif for a sunny day or any occasion when you want a refreshing drink with a twist.

NOTES

Syrah Chicken & Bacon Roll-Ups

APPETIZER

Syrah Wine Chicken & Bacon Roll-Ups are a savory and indulgent dish that combines tender chicken breasts, smoky bacon, and a flavorful Syrah wine reduction sauce. This gourmet meal is perfect for a special dinner, impressing guests, or simply treating yourself to a culinary delight. Makes 4 servings.

Ingredients:

- 4 boneless, skinless chicken breasts
- 8 slices of bacon
- Salt and black pepper to taste
- 2 tablespoons olive oil
- 1 cup Syrah wine
- 1/2 cup chicken broth
- 2 cloves garlic, minced
- 1 tablespoon fresh rosemary, chopped
- 1 tablespoon fresh thyme, chopped

Instructions:

1. Preheat the Oven:
Preheat your oven to 375°F (190°C).

2. Flatten Chicken Breasts:
Place each chicken breast between two sheets of plastic wrap and gently pound them to an even thickness of about 1/2 inch. Season with salt and black pepper.

3. Roll the Chicken:
Lay a slice of bacon on top of each chicken breast and roll them up, securing with toothpicks.

4. Sear the Chicken:
In a large oven-safe skillet, heat the olive oil over medium-high heat. Add the chicken roll-ups and sear on all sides until the bacon is crispy, about 2-3 minutes per side. Remove the chicken from the skillet and set it aside.

5. Prepare the Syrah Wine Reduction:
In the same skillet, add the minced garlic, chopped rosemary, and thyme. Sauté for about 1 minute until fragrant. Pour in the Syrah wine and chicken broth, scraping up any browned bits from the bottom of the skillet. Allow the sauce to simmer and reduce by half, about 5-7 minutes. If desired, whisk in a tablespoon of butter for added richness.

6. Bake:
Return the seared chicken roll-ups to the skillet, coating them with the Syrah wine reduction. Place the skillet in the preheated oven and bake for 15-20 minutes or until the chicken reaches an internal temperature of 165°F (74°C).

7. Serve:
Remove the toothpicks from the chicken roll-ups before serving. Spoon the delicious Syrah wine reduction sauce over the top.

NOTES

Syrah Blue Cheese Logs

APPETIZER

Elevate your cheese platter with these elegant Syrah-infused Blue Cheese Logs. Creamy, tangy blue cheese rolled in aromatic herbs and crushed black peppercorns, then lightly soaked in Syrah wine for a delightful twist. Makes 2 logs, each serving 8-10 people.

Ingredients:

For the Blue Cheese Logs:
- 12 ounces (about 1 1/2 cups) quality blue cheese, crumbled
- 4 ounces cream cheese, softened
- 1/4 cup finely chopped fresh chives
- 1/4 cup fresh thyme leaves
- 1/4 cup fresh rosemary leaves, finely chopped
- 2 teaspoons black peppercorns, crushed

For the Syrah Infusion:
- 1 cup Syrah wine
- 1/4 cup honey

For Coating:
- Crushed black peppercorns
- Fresh herbs (thyme, rosemary) for garnish

INSTRUCTIONS:

1. Prepare the Blue Cheese Mixture:
In a mixing bowl, combine the crumbled blue cheese, softened cream cheese, finely chopped chives, fresh thyme leaves, and finely chopped fresh rosemary. Mix until all ingredients are well incorporated.

2. Shape the Logs:
Divide the cheese mixture into two equal portions. Lay out two sheets of plastic wrap, and on each, form one portion of the cheese mixture into a log shape. Roll the logs tightly in plastic wrap, ensuring they are well-formed and compact. Refrigerate for at least 1 hour, or until firm.

3. Prepare the Syrah Infusion:
In a small saucepan, heat the Syrah wine and honey over low heat, stirring until the honey dissolves. Remove from heat and let it cool to room temperature.

4. Soak the Logs:
Unwrap the chilled cheese logs and place them in a shallow dish. Pour the cooled Syrah and honey mixture over the logs, allowing them to soak for about 30 minutes, turning occasionally for even coverage.

5. Coat with Peppercorns:
After soaking, remove the logs from the Syrah mixture and roll them in the crushed black peppercorns, coating them evenly. Press the peppercorns gently to adhere.

6. Chill Again:
Re-wrap the logs in plastic wrap and refrigerate for an additional 30 minutes to firm up.

7. Serve:
Before serving, garnish with fresh thyme and rosemary leaves. Slice and serve with your favorite crackers, bread, or fruit.

NOTES

Syrah Braised Baby Artichokes

SIDE DISH

This delightful dish features tender baby artichokes braised to perfection in Syrah wine, creating a harmonious blend of flavors. Served with a vibrant tomato coulis, it's a taste of Mediterranean cuisine in every bite. Makes 4 servings.

Ingredients:

For the Braised Baby Artichokes:
- 12 baby artichokes
- 2 cups Syrah wine
- 2 cups vegetable broth
- 4 cloves garlic, minced
- 1 lemon, juiced
- 2 sprigs fresh thyme
- 2 sprigs fresh rosemary
- Salt and black pepper to taste
- Olive oil for sautéing

For the Tomato Coulis:
- 4 large tomatoes, diced
- 1 onion, chopped
- 2 cloves garlic, minced
- 1/4 cup tomato paste
- 1/4 cup Syrah wine
- 2 tablespoons olive oil
- 1 teaspoon dried oregano
- Salt and black pepper to taste
- Fresh basil leaves for garnish

Instructions:

Prepare the Baby Artichokes:

1. Begin by trimming the baby artichokes. Remove tough outer leaves, trim the tops, and cut them in half lengthwise. Place them in a bowl of water with lemon juice to prevent browning.
2. In a large skillet or Dutch oven, heat olive oil over medium-high heat. Add minced garlic and sauté until fragrant.
3. Drain the artichokes and add them to the skillet. Sauté for about 5 minutes until they start to brown.
4. Pour in Syrah wine and vegetable broth. Add fresh thyme and rosemary sprigs. Season with salt and black pepper. Bring to a simmer.
5. Cover and let the artichokes braise for about 30-40 minutes until they are tender and flavorful. Check the liquid level and add more vegetable broth if needed.

Prepare the Tomato Coulis:

6. While the artichokes are braising, heat olive oil in a separate pan over medium heat. Add chopped onions and garlic. Sauté until translucent.
7. Stir in diced tomatoes and cook for about 5 minutes until they begin to break down.
8. Add tomato paste, Syrah wine, dried oregano, salt, and black pepper. Cook for an additional 10-15 minutes, allowing the flavors to meld. If needed, add a bit of water to reach your desired consistency.

Serve:

9. To serve, spoon onto plates and drizzle with the Tomato Coulis. Garnish with fresh basil leaves for a burst of color and freshness.

Notes

Syrah

Green Beans Almondine

SIDE DISH

Syrah Wine Green Beans Almondine is a delightful side dish that elevates tender green beans with the nutty crunch of toasted almonds and the rich depth of Syrah wine. It's a perfect accompaniment to any meal. Makes 4 servings.

Ingredients:

- 1 pound fresh green beans, trimmed
- 1/2 cup sliced almonds
- 2 tablespoons unsalted butter
- 1/4 cup Syrah wine
- 1 tablespoon olive oil
- 2 cloves garlic, minced
- Zest of 1 lemon
- Salt and black pepper to taste
- Lemon wedges for garnish (optional)

Instructions:

1. Blanch the Green Beans:
Bring a large pot of salted water to a boil. Add the green beans and cook for about 2-3 minutes until they turn bright green and are crisp-tender. Immediately drain and transfer the beans to a bowl of ice water to stop the cooking process. Drain again and set aside.

2. Toast the Almonds:
In a dry skillet over medium heat, toast the sliced almonds until they become golden and fragrant, about 3-4 minutes. Keep a close eye on them to prevent burning. Transfer the toasted almonds to a plate and set aside.

3. Sauté the Garlic:
In the same skillet, add the olive oil and minced garlic. Sauté for about 30 seconds until the garlic becomes fragrant but not browned.

4. Add the Green Beans:
Add the blanched green beans to the skillet with the garlic. Sauté for 2-3 minutes, tossing them in the oil and garlic until heated through.

5. Deglaze with Syrah Wine:
Pour the Syrah wine over the green beans. Stir and cook for 1-2 minutes until the wine has reduced slightly and coated the beans.

6. Add Butter and Lemon Zest:
Add the unsalted butter and lemon zest to the skillet. Stir until the butter has melted, coating the beans with a rich, citrusy sauce. Season with salt and black pepper to taste.

7. Serve:
Transfer to a serving platter. Sprinkle the toasted almonds evenly over the top. Garnish with lemon wedges if desired. Serve immediately as a flavorful side dish.

Notes

Syrah Coq au Vin

MAIN COURSE

Syrah Wine Coq au Vin is a classic French dish with a twist. Succulent chicken, mushrooms, and pearl onions are simmered in a rich Syrah wine sauce until tender and bursting with flavor. Makes 4-6 servings.

Ingredients:

- 4 slices bacon, chopped
- 4 chicken legs (thigh and drumstick), skin-on
- Salt and black pepper to taste
- 1 cup pearl onions, peeled
- 8 ounces mushrooms, sliced
- 3 cloves garlic, minced
- 2 cups Syrah wine
- 1 cup chicken broth
- 2 tablespoons tomato paste
- 2 sprigs fresh thyme
- 2 bay leaves
- 2 tablespoons butter
- 2 tablespoons all-purpose flour
- Chopped fresh parsley for garnish

Instructions:

Cook the Bacon:
1. In a large, heavy-bottomed pot or Dutch oven, cook the chopped bacon over medium heat until it becomes crispy. Remove the bacon with a slotted spoon and set it aside, leaving the bacon fat in the pot.

Brown the Chicken:
2. Season the chicken legs with salt and black pepper. In the same pot with the bacon fat, sear the chicken over medium-high heat until it's browned on all sides. Remove the chicken from the pot and set it aside.

Sauté the Vegetables:
3. In the same pot, add the pearl onions and mushrooms. Sauté for about 5 minutes until they start to brown. Add the minced garlic and cook for another minute.

Deglaze with Wine:
4. Pour in the Syrah wine and scrape up any browned bits from the bottom of the pot with a wooden spoon. Allow the wine to simmer for about 5 minutes to reduce slightly.

Add Broth and Flavorings:
5. Stir in the chicken broth, tomato paste, fresh thyme sprigs, bay leaves, and the reserved cooked bacon. Return the browned chicken to the pot.

6. Cover the pot and simmer over low heat for about 45 minutes to 1 hour, or until the chicken is tender and cooked through.

Make the Roux:
7. In a small saucepan, melt the butter over medium heat. Stir in the flour and cook for 1-2 minutes until it forms a smooth paste (roux). Remove from heat.

Thicken the Sauce:
8. Remove the cooked chicken, onions, mushrooms, and herbs from the pot. Discard the bay leaves and thyme sprigs.

9. Stir the roux into the simmering sauce in the pot. Cook for a few minutes until the sauce thickens.

Combine and Serve:
10. Return the chicken, mushrooms, and onions to the pot. Simmer for an additional 10-15 minutes until everything is heated through.

11. Serve hot, garnished with chopped fresh parsley.

Syrah
Chicken & Mushroom Fricassee

MAIN COURSE

Syrah Wine Chicken and Mushroom Fricassee is a comforting French classic with a twist. Tender chicken and sautéed mushrooms are bathed in a velvety Syrah wine sauce, creating a hearty and elegant dish. Makes 4 servings.

Ingredients:

- 4 bone-in, skin-on chicken thighs
- Salt and black pepper to taste
- 2 tablespoons olive oil
- 8 ounces mushrooms, sliced
- 1 onion, finely chopped
- 2 cloves garlic, minced
- 1 cup Syrah wine
- 1 cup chicken broth
- 2 sprigs fresh thyme
- 2 bay leaves
- 2 tablespoons butter
- 2 tablespoons all-purpose flour
- Chopped fresh parsley for garnish

Instructions:

Brown the Chicken:
1. Season the chicken thighs with salt and black pepper. In a large, heavy skillet or Dutch oven, heat the olive oil over medium-high heat. Add the chicken thighs, skin-side down, and cook until they are well-browned, about 5 minutes per side. Remove the chicken from the skillet and set it aside.

Sauté the Vegetables:
2. In the same skillet, add the sliced mushrooms and cook for about 5 minutes until they start to brown. Add the chopped onion and garlic, cooking for an additional 2 minutes until fragrant.

Deglaze with Wine:
3. Pour in the Syrah wine, stirring to scrape up any browned bits from the bottom of the skillet. Allow the wine to simmer for about 5 minutes until it reduces slightly.

Add Broth and Flavorings:
4. Stir in the chicken broth, fresh thyme sprigs, and bay leaves. Return the browned chicken thighs to the skillet.
5. Cover the skillet and simmer over low heat for about 20-25 minutes, or until the chicken is cooked through and tender.

Make the Roux:
6. In a small saucepan, melt the butter over medium heat. Stir in the flour and cook for 1-2 minutes until it forms a smooth paste (roux). Remove from heat.

Thicken the Sauce:
7. Remove the chicken and herbs from the skillet. Discard the bay leaves and thyme sprigs.
8. Stir the roux into the simmering sauce in the skillet. Cook for a few minutes until the sauce thickens and becomes velvety.

Combine and Serve:
9. Return the chicken and mushrooms to the skillet. Simmer for an additional 5 minutes to heat everything through.
10. Serve hot, garnished with chopped fresh parsley. This dish pairs wonderfully with mashed potatoes, rice, or crusty bread to soak up the delicious Syrah wine sauce. Enjoy!

Notes

Syrah Short Rib Bourguignon

MAIN COURSE

Syrah Wine Short Rib Bourguignon is a rich and hearty French classic. Tender braised short ribs are bathed in a luscious Syrah wine sauce with mushrooms and pearl onions, creating a savory and indulgent dish. Makes 4 servings.

Ingredients:

- 4 bone-in beef short ribs
- Salt and black pepper to taste
- 2 tablespoons olive oil
- 1 onion, chopped
- 2 carrots, chopped
- 2 cloves garlic, minced
- 8 ounces mushrooms, sliced
- 1 cup pearl onions, peeled
- 2 cups Syrah wine
- 1 cup beef broth
- 2 sprigs fresh thyme
- 2 bay leaves
- 2 tablespoons tomato paste
- 2 tablespoons all-purpose flour
- Chopped fresh parsley for garnish

INSTRUCTIONS:

Brown the Short Ribs:
1. Season the short ribs with salt and black pepper. In a large Dutch oven or heavy skillet, heat the olive oil over medium-high heat. Add the short ribs and brown them on all sides, about 5 minutes per side. Remove the short ribs and set them aside.

Sauté the Vegetables:
2. In the same pot, add the chopped onion and carrots. Sauté for about 5 minutes until they begin to soften. Add the minced garlic and sliced mushrooms, cooking for an additional 2 minutes.

Deglaze with Wine:
3. Pour in the Syrah wine, stirring to scrape up any browned bits from the bottom of the pot. Allow the wine to simmer for about 10 minutes until it reduces by half.

Add Broth and Flavorings:
4. Stir in the beef broth, fresh thyme sprigs, bay leaves, and tomato paste. Return the browned short ribs to the pot.
5. Cover the pot and simmer over low heat for 2.5 to 3 hours, or until the short ribs are tender and can be easily pulled apart.

Make the Roux:
6. In a small saucepan, melt 2 tablespoons of butter over medium heat. Stir in 2 tablespoons of all-purpose flour to create a smooth paste (roux). Remove from heat.

Thicken the Sauce:
7. Remove the short ribs and discard the thyme sprigs and bay leaves.
8. Stir the roux into the simmering sauce in the pot. Cook for a few minutes until the sauce thickens and becomes rich and velvety.

Combine and Serve:
9. Return the short ribs, add the pearl onions, and simmer for an additional 10-15 minutes until everything is heated through.
10. Serve hot, garnished with chopped fresh parsley.

NOTES

Syrah Ratatouille

MAIN COURSE

Syrah Wine Ratatouille is a classic Provencal dish elevated by the deep, rich flavors of Syrah wine. This hearty vegetable medley is slow-cooked to perfection, creating a deliciously aromatic and savory masterpiece. Makes 6 servings.

Ingredients:

- 1 large eggplant, diced
- 2 zucchinis, diced
- 2 yellow bell peppers, diced
- 1 red onion, chopped
- 4 cloves garlic, minced
- 2 cups crushed tomatoes
- 1/2 cup Syrah wine
- 2 sprigs fresh thyme
- 2 sprigs fresh rosemary
- 2 bay leaves
- Salt and black pepper to taste
- Olive oil for sautéing
- Chopped fresh basil for garnish

INSTRUCTIONS:

Sauté the Vegetables:

1. In a large skillet or Dutch oven, heat a few tablespoons of olive oil over medium-high heat. Add the diced eggplant and zucchini. Sauté until they start to brown, about 5 minutes. Remove and set aside.

2. In the same skillet, add more olive oil if needed. Add the diced bell peppers, chopped red onion, and minced garlic. Sauté until softened, about 5 minutes.

Combine and Simmer:

3. Return the sautéed eggplant and zucchini to the skillet. Stir in the crushed tomatoes, Syrah wine, fresh thyme sprigs, fresh rosemary sprigs, and bay leaves.

4. Season the mixture with salt and black pepper to taste. Mix well.

5. Cover the skillet and reduce the heat to low. Let the Ratatouille simmer for about 30-40 minutes, stirring occasionally, until all the vegetables are tender and the flavors meld together.

Serve:

6. Once done, remove the bay leaves, thyme sprigs, and rosemary sprigs.

7. Serve hot, garnished with freshly chopped basil. This dish pairs wonderfully with crusty bread, pasta, or as a side to grilled meats.

NOTES

Syrah Cherry Flaugnarde

DESSERT

Syrah Wine Cherry Flaugnarde is a rustic French dessert that combines the rich and fruity flavors of Syrah wine with sweet cherries. This custardy treat is easy to make and perfect for showcasing the deep notes of Syrah. Makes one 9-inch flaugnarde, serving 6-8.

Ingredients:

- 1 cup fresh or frozen sweet cherries, pitted
- 3 large eggs
- 1/2 cup granulated sugar
- 1/2 cup all-purpose flour
- 1 cup whole milk
- 1/4 cup Syrah wine
- 1 teaspoon vanilla extract
- 1/4 teaspoon almond extract (optional)
- Powdered sugar, for dusting

INSTRUCTIONS:

1. Preheat the Oven:
Preheat your oven to 350°F (175°C). Grease a 9-inch round baking dish.

2. Prepare the Cherries:
If using fresh cherries, pit them and set aside. If using frozen cherries, make sure they are thawed and drained.

3. Whisk the Batter:
In a mixing bowl, whisk together the eggs and granulated sugar until well combined and slightly frothy. Add the flour, milk, Syrah wine, vanilla extract, and almond extract (if using). Whisk until you have a smooth batter.

4. Layer the Cherries:
Place the pitted cherries in the greased baking dish, spreading them evenly.

5. Pour the Batter:
Pour the batter over the cherries. The cherries may float to the top; this is normal.

6. Bake:
Place the baking dish in the preheated oven and bake for 40-45 minutes, or until the flaugnarde is set and the top is golden brown. It should puff up while baking.

7. Cool and Dust:
Remove the flaugnarde from the oven and let it cool slightly. It will deflate as it cools. Dust the top with powdered sugar before serving.

8. Serve:
Traditionally served warm or at room temperature. Slice and enjoy this delightful dessert with a glass of Syrah wine.

NOTES

Syrah S.H.P.C Tarte Tatin

DESSERT

This Syrah Wine **Salted Honey, Pear, and Chocolate** Tarte Tatin is a decadent dessert that combines the deep richness of Syrah wine with the sweetness of pears, the indulgence of chocolate, and the perfect touch of salt. It's a show-stopping treat that's surprisingly easy to make. Makes one 9-inch tarte Tatin, serving 6-8.

Ingredients:

For the Tarte Tatin:

- 4-5 ripe pears, peeled, cored, and halved
- 1/2 cup granulated sugar
- 1/4 cup salted butter
- 2 tablespoons Syrah wine
- 1 sheet of puff pastry (store-bought or homemade)

For the Salted Honey Chocolate Sauce:

- 1/2 cup heavy cream
- 1/2 cup dark chocolate chips
- 2 tablespoons salted honey
- Pinch of sea salt

Instructions:

Prepare the Tarte Tatin:

1. Preheat the Oven: Preheat your oven to 375°F (190°C).

2. Caramelize the Sugar: In a 9-inch ovenproof skillet or Tarte Tatin dish, sprinkle the granulated sugar evenly. Heat it over medium-high heat until it begins to melt and turn golden. Swirl the pan occasionally to ensure even caramelization.

3. Add Butter and Pears: Add the salted butter to the caramelized sugar and stir until melted. Place the pear halves, rounded side down, into the caramel, fitting them snugly. Cook for a few minutes until the pears start to soften and caramelize slightly.

4. Deglaze with Syrah Wine: Drizzle the Syrah wine over the pears and caramel. Allow it to simmer for a minute or two to intensify the flavor.

5. Cover with Puff Pastry: Roll out the puff pastry to fit the size of your skillet or dish. Lay it over the pears, tucking the edges down around the pears.

6. Bake: Transfer the skillet or dish to the preheated oven and bake for 25-30 minutes or until the pastry is golden brown and puffed.

Prepare the Salted Honey Chocolate Sauce:

1. Heat the Cream: In a small saucepan, heat the heavy cream over medium heat until it begins to simmer. Remove it from the heat.

2. Melt the Chocolate: Add the dark chocolate chips to the hot cream and let them sit for a minute to soften. Stir until the chocolate is completely melted and the mixture is smooth.

3. Add Honey and Salt: Stir in the salted honey and a pinch of sea salt to taste. The salt should balance the sweetness of the sauce.

Assemble and Serve:

1. Cool Slightly: Let the tarte Tatin cool in the skillet or dish for about 10 minutes.

2. Invert onto a Plate: Place a serving plate over the skillet or dish, and with oven mitts or a towel, carefully and quickly invert the tarte Tatin onto the plate. Be cautious as the caramel may still be hot.

3. Serve Warm: Slice and serve while it's still warm, drizzled with the salted honey chocolate sauce. Enjoy with a glass of Syrah wine for the perfect pairing.

VIOGNIER
Wine Notes

~ Food Pairing Suggestions ~

Seafood: Viognier's fruity and floral qualities make it an excellent match for seafood, especially dishes with buttery or creamy sauces, like lobster bisque or shrimp scampi.

Poultry: It complements poultry dishes, particularly those with fruit-based or creamy sauces, such as chicken in a peach glaze.

Spicy Cuisine: Viognier's lush fruitiness can temper the heat in spicy dishes, such as Thai or Indian cuisine.

Pork: It pairs well with pork dishes, including roast pork with apricot glaze or honey mustard.

Mild Cheeses: Enjoy it with mild, soft cheeses like brie or camembert.

Asian Cuisine: Viognier complements the flavors of Asian cuisine, particularly dishes with ginger or lemongrass.

Salads: It's a refreshing choice for salads with fruit components, such as a mixed greens salad with peaches and goat cheese.

Creamy Pasta: Viognier's richness enhances creamy pasta dishes, like fettuccine Alfredo.

Duck: It pairs wonderfully with duck dishes, especially those with a fruit-based sauce like orange duck.

Desserts: Viognier can be paired with dessert courses featuring fruit-based pastries or light, fruity cakes.

PRIMARY FLAVORS
~

Stone Fruits:
Viognier is celebrated for its lush, aromatic flavors of ripe stone fruits, including apricot, peach, and nectarine.

Floral Bouquet:
It often boasts floral notes, particularly honeysuckle, orange blossom, and sometimes jasmine.

Citrus Accents:
Viognier can feature subtle citrus flavors like tangerine or lemon zest, adding brightness.

Spices and Herbs:
Depending on the region and winemaking style, you may detect hints of spices like ginger or herbs like basil.

TASTE PROFILE
~

Body:
Viognier typically has a medium to full body, offering a rich and rounded mouthfeel.

Acidity:
Viognier's acidity can vary, but it often has a moderate to high level, providing balance.

Alcohol:
It often has a moderate to high alcohol content, contributing to its richness and warmth.

Finish:
Viognier often has a long and aromatic finish, with lingering fruit and floral notes.

Chapter Seven
Viognier

Welcome to a culinary journey through the world of Viognier wine. Known for its elegant aromas and versatility, Viognier is a grape varietal that offers a myriad of possibilities for the creative cook. In this chapter, we'll uncover the unique qualities that make Viognier an ideal companion in the kitchen, from its enchanting floral bouquet to its luscious stone fruit flavors.

Viognier's signature qualities lie in its enchanting fragrance. As you explore the world of Viognier-infused dishes, you'll discover how its aromatic notes of white flowers, apricots, and peaches can elevate both sweet and savory recipes. From delicate seafood to rich, creamy sauces, Viognier has the ability to enhance flavors and add a touch of sophistication to your culinary creations.

So, whether you're a seasoned chef or an adventurous home cook, join us on this culinary odyssey as we uncover the secrets of Viognier wine and its extraordinary potential in the world of gastronomy. From appetizers to desserts, you'll find that Viognier is a versatile and inspiring ingredient that adds a touch of elegance to every dish.

Viognier Vodka Elixir

COCKTAIL

The Viognier Vodka Elixir is a smooth and aromatic cocktail that blends the crisp purity of Viognier wine with the clear spirits of vodka. It's a delightful elixir that's perfect for those who enjoy a nuanced and refreshing drink. Makes one cocktail, easily scalable for multiple servings.

Ingredients:

- 2 oz Viognier wine
- 1 oz vodka
- 1/2 oz elderflower liqueur (optional)
- 1/2 oz fresh lemon juice
- 1/4 oz simple syrup (adjust to taste)
- Ice cubes
- Lemon twist or edible flowers for garnish (optional)

INSTRUCTIONS:

1. Chill Your Glass:
Place a stemmed wine glass or coupe glass in the freezer to chill.

2. Prepare the Cocktail:
In a cocktail shaker filled with ice, combine the Viognier wine, vodka, elderflower liqueur (if using), fresh lemon juice, and simple syrup.

3. Shake Well:
Shake the mixture vigorously for about 10-15 seconds to thoroughly chill and blend the ingredients.

4. Strain and Serve:
Remove the chilled glass from the freezer and strain the cocktail into it.

5. Garnish:
If desired, garnish your Viognier Vodka Elixir with a lemon twist or a delicate edible flower.

NOTES

Viognier Visions
COCKTAIL

Viognier Visions is an enchanting cocktail that combines the aromatic charm of Viognier wine with the mysterious allure of absinthe. It's a captivating concoction for those who appreciate a touch of the extraordinary in their drinks. Makes one cocktail, easily scalable for multiple servings.

Ingredients:

- 2 oz Viognier wine
- 1/2 oz absinthe
- 1/2 oz simple syrup (adjust to taste)
- 1 dash orange bitters
- Ice cubes
- Orange twist or star anise for garnish (optional)

Instructions:

1. Chill Your Glass:
Place a stemmed wine glass or coupe glass in the freezer to chill.

2. Prepare the Cocktail:
In a mixing glass filled with ice, combine the Viognier wine, absinthe, simple syrup, and a dash of orange bitters.

3. Stir Well:
Stir the mixture gently for about 15-20 seconds. This chills the ingredients and ensures proper blending.

4. Strain and Serve:
Remove the chilled glass from the freezer and strain the cocktail into it.

5. Garnish:
If desired, garnish your Viognier Visions with a twist of orange peel or a single star anise for a touch of mystique.

Notes

Viognier
Scallops with Citrus Drizzle

APPETIZER

Elevate your appetizer game with these succulent scallops glazed with a Viognier wine reduction and garnished with a zesty citrus drizzle. A perfect blend of sweet and tangy flavors. Makes 4 servings.

Ingredients:

For the Viognier Glaze:
- 1 cup Viognier wine
- 1/4 cup honey
- 2 tablespoons fresh orange juice
- 1 teaspoon orange zest
- 1 teaspoon fresh lemon juice
- 1 teaspoon fresh lime juice
- Salt and black pepper, to taste

For the Scallops:
- 12 large sea scallops, cleaned and patted dry
- Salt and black pepper, to taste
- 2 tablespoons olive oil

For the Citrus Drizzle:
- 1/4 cup fresh orange juice
- 1 tablespoon fresh lemon juice
- 1 tablespoon fresh lime juice
- 1 tablespoon extra-virgin olive oil
- 1 teaspoon honey
- Salt and black pepper, to taste

Garnish:
- Fresh cilantro or parsley leaves
- Citrus zest (orange, lemon, or lime)

INSTRUCTIONS:

For the Viognier Glaze:

1. In a saucepan, combine the Viognier wine, honey, orange juice, orange zest, lemon juice, and lime juice.

2. Season with a pinch of salt and black pepper to taste.

3. Bring the mixture to a boil over medium-high heat, then reduce the heat to a simmer.

4. Allow it to simmer for about 15-20 minutes or until the glaze thickens and reduces by half. Remove from heat and set aside.

For the Scallops:

1. Season the scallops with a pinch of salt and black pepper.

2. In a large skillet, heat the olive oil over medium-high heat until it shimmers.

3. Carefully add the scallops to the skillet, making sure they are not crowded. Cook for about 2-3 minutes on each side, or until they develop a golden sear and are just cooked through.

For the Citrus Drizzle:

1. In a small bowl, whisk together the fresh orange juice, lemon juice, lime juice, extra-virgin olive oil, honey, salt, and black pepper until well combined.

To Serve:

Spoon a portion of the Viognier glaze onto each plate. Place three seared scallops on each plate, over the glaze. Drizzle the citrus mixture over the scallops. Garnish with fresh cilantro or parsley leaves and citrus zest.

NOTES

Viognier
Olive Tapenade
APPETIZER

Viognier Wine Olive Tapenade is a savory and tangy spread bursting with the flavors of olives, capers, and anchovies, elevated with the subtle notes of Viognier wine. This Mediterranean-inspired condiment is perfect for spreading on crusty bread, crackers, or as a flavorful addition to various dishes. Makes approximately 1 cup of tapenade.

Ingredients:

- 1 cup pitted Kalamata olives
- 1/4 cup capers, drained
- 2 cloves garlic, minced
- 2 anchovy fillets (optional), minced
- 2 tablespoons fresh lemon juice
- 2 tablespoons Viognier wine
- 2 tablespoons extra-virgin olive oil
- 1 teaspoon fresh thyme leaves (or 1/2 teaspoon dried thyme)
- Freshly ground black pepper, to taste

INSTRUCTIONS:

1. Prepare the Ingredients:
Ensure the olives are pitted, and if using anchovy fillets, mince them finely. Drain the capers.

2. Combine in a Food Processor:
In a food processor, combine the pitted Kalamata olives, capers, minced garlic, minced anchovy fillets (if using), fresh lemon juice, Viognier wine, extra-virgin olive oil, and fresh thyme leaves.

3. Process Until Smooth:
Pulse the ingredients until they form a coarse paste. You can adjust the texture to your preference by processing it for a shorter or longer time. Some people prefer a chunkier tapenade, while others prefer it smoother.

4. Taste and Season:
Taste the Viognier Wine Olive Tapenade and add freshly ground black pepper as needed. Depending on the saltiness of your olives and capers, you may not need to add additional salt.

5. Transfer and Store:
Spoon the tapenade into an airtight container or a small serving bowl. If not serving immediately, cover and refrigerate. It can be stored in the refrigerator for up to a week.

6. Serve:
Serve as a spread on slices of baguette, crackers, or alongside a cheese platter. It also makes a delightful topping for grilled chicken, fish, or pasta dishes, adding a burst of Mediterranean flavor to your meal.

NOTES

Viognier Fondant Potatoes

SIDE DISH

Viognier Wine Fondant Potatoes are a luxurious and indulgent side dish. Creamy on the inside with a golden, crispy exterior, they're elevated to perfection with the addition of aromatic Viognier wine. Makes 4 servings.

Ingredients:

- 4 large russet potatoes, peeled and cut into cylinders
- 1/4 cup unsalted butter
- 1/4 cup Viognier wine
- 1/4 cup chicken or vegetable broth
- 2 cloves garlic, minced
- 2 sprigs fresh thyme
- Salt and black pepper to taste
- Chopped fresh parsley for garnish

INSTRUCTIONS:

1. Preheat your oven to 400°F (200°C).

Prepare the Potatoes:

2. In a large skillet or frying pan, melt the butter over medium-high heat. Add the potato cylinders and sear until they turn a beautiful golden brown on all sides, about 5-7 minutes.

3. Reduce the heat to low and add the minced garlic and fresh thyme sprigs. Sauté for another minute until the garlic is fragrant.

4. Pour in the Viognier wine and chicken or vegetable broth. Season with salt and black pepper. Bring the mixture to a simmer.

Bake the Potatoes:

5. Transfer the skillet or frying pan to the preheated oven. Bake for 30-35 minutes, basting the potatoes with the liquid every 10-15 minutes. This will help create that delectable crispy exterior.

6. Once the potatoes are tender on the inside and golden and crispy on the outside, remove them from the oven.

Serve:

7. Transfer to a serving dish, drizzling them with the flavorful cooking liquid. Remove the thyme sprigs.

8. Garnish with chopped fresh parsley for a burst of color and freshness.

NOTES

Viognier Spinach au Gratin

SIDE DISH

Viognier Wine Spinach au Gratin is a delightful side dish that combines the earthy richness of spinach with the creamy decadence of a cheese sauce infused with aromatic Viognier wine. Topped with a golden breadcrumb crust, it's comfort food with a touch of elegance. Makes 4-6 servings.

Ingredients:

- 1 pound fresh spinach, washed and trimmed
- 1/4 cup unsalted butter
- 1/4 cup all-purpose flour
- 1 cup Viognier wine
- 1 cup milk
- 1 cup shredded Gruyère cheese
- 1/2 cup grated Parmesan cheese
- 1/2 teaspoon nutmeg
- Salt and black pepper to taste
- 1/2 cup breadcrumbs
- 2 tablespoons melted butter
- Chopped fresh parsley for garnish

INSTRUCTIONS:

Prepare the Spinach:
1. In a large pot, bring salted water to a boil. Add the fresh spinach and blanch for 2 minutes. Drain and rinse the spinach under cold water to stop the cooking process. Squeeze out excess moisture and chop the spinach coarsely.

Make the Cheese Sauce:
2. In a saucepan over medium heat, melt 1/4 cup of unsalted butter. Add the flour and whisk continuously for about 2 minutes to create a roux.

3. Slowly pour in the Viognier wine, whisking constantly until the mixture thickens and becomes smooth.

4. Gradually add the milk while continuing to whisk. Cook for another 5 minutes, or until the sauce has thickened.

5. Stir in the shredded Gruyère cheese and grated Parmesan cheese. Continue to cook and stir until the cheese has melted into the sauce and it's smooth and creamy.

6. Season the sauce with nutmeg, salt, and black pepper to taste.

Assemble and Bake:
7. Preheat your oven to 375°F (190°C).

8. In a greased baking dish, spread the chopped spinach evenly.

9. Pour the Viognier wine cheese sauce over the spinach, ensuring it's well-distributed.

10. In a small bowl, combine the breadcrumbs with 2 tablespoons of melted butter. Sprinkle this breadcrumb mixture evenly over the spinach and sauce.

Bake and Serve:
11. Place the baking dish in the preheated oven and bake for approximately 20-25 minutes or until the top is golden and the sauce is bubbling.

12. Once done, remove from the oven and let it cool for a few minutes.

13. Garnish with chopped fresh parsley.

14. Serve this creamy, wine-infused spinach au gratin as a side dish to complement your meal.

NOTES

GUEST RECIPE

Viognier
Pan-Seared Salmon
with Lemon Herb Vegetables — MAIN COURSE

Indulge in the exquisite flavors of pan-seared salmon paired with tender yellow squash and vibrant peas in this delightful dish. Finished with a squeeze of lemon and a sprinkle of fresh herbs, it's a light and flavorful meal perfectly complemented by a glass of Ramona Ranch Viognier or Sangiovese. Recipe from Micole Moore at Ramona Ranch Vineyard & Winery.

Ingredients:

- 1/2 lb salmon fillet
- Saltwater brine (for submerging salmon)
- 1 tablespoon extra virgin olive oil (EVOO)
- 1/2 cup diced yellow squash
- 1/4 cup frozen peas
- Lemon wedge (for garnish)
- Fresh herbs (for garnish)

Instructions:

1. Prepare the Salmon
Submerge the salmon in a saltwater brine for 15 minutes before cooking; then pat it dry.

2. Cook the Salmon
Heat EVOO in a cast-iron pan, place the salmon skin side down, and cook for approximately 6 minutes, depending on thickness and desired doneness. Flip the salmon over, add diced yellow squash to the pan on the side of the salmon, and cook for 3 more minutes. Then, add frozen peas, cover the pan, and cook for approximately 2 more minutes or until the salmon flakes easily, which is a great indicator of doneness.

3. Plate the Salmon
Plate the salmon and vegetables, serve with a lemon wedge on the side, and garnish with fresh herbs from your garden.

4. Serve
Pair with Ramona Ranch Viognier or Sangiovese for a delightful meal.

Notes

Viognier Chicken Française

MAIN COURSE

Viognier Wine Chicken Française is an elegant and flavorful dish featuring tender chicken cutlets bathed in a luscious lemon and Viognier wine sauce. This classic French-inspired recipe is perfect for a special dinner and pairs beautifully with a glass of Viognier wine. Makes 4 servings.

Ingredients:

For the Chicken:
- 4 boneless, skinless chicken breasts, pounded to an even thickness
- Salt and freshly ground black pepper, to taste
- 1 cup all-purpose flour, for dredging
- 2 large eggs
- 2 tablespoons water
- 1/4 cup grated Parmesan cheese
- 2 tablespoons olive oil
- 2 tablespoons unsalted butter

For the Lemon Viognier Wine Sauce:
- 1/2 cup Viognier wine
- 1/2 cup chicken broth
- Juice of 2 lemons
- 1/4 cup fresh parsley, chopped
- 2 cloves garlic, minced
- 2 tablespoons unsalted butter
- Salt and freshly ground black pepper, to taste
- Lemon slices and additional parsley for garnish (optional)

Instructions:

1. Prepare the Chicken:
Season the chicken breasts with salt and freshly ground black pepper. Dredge each chicken breast in flour, shaking off any excess.

2. Prepare the Egg Mixture:
In a shallow bowl, whisk together the eggs, water, and grated Parmesan cheese.

3. Coat the Chicken:
Heat the olive oil and butter in a large skillet over medium-high heat. Dip each flour-coated chicken breast into the egg mixture, allowing any excess to drip off, and then place it in the hot skillet. Cook for about 3-4 minutes on each side, or until the chicken is golden brown and cooked through. Remove the chicken from the skillet and place it on a plate. Keep warm.

4. Make the Lemon Viognier Wine Sauce:
In the same skillet, add minced garlic and cook for about 30 seconds until fragrant. Pour in the Viognier wine, chicken broth, and lemon juice. Use a wooden spoon to scrape up any browned bits from the bottom of the skillet. Simmer for about 5-7 minutes, or until the sauce reduces slightly.

5. Finish the Sauce:
Reduce the heat to low and add 2 tablespoons of butter to the sauce, stirring until it melts and thickens the sauce. Season with salt and freshly ground black pepper to taste. Stir in the chopped fresh parsley.

6. Serve:
Return the cooked chicken breasts to the skillet, allowing them to warm briefly in the sauce. Spoon the lemon Viognier wine sauce over the chicken.

7. Garnish and Serve:
Optionally, garnish with lemon slices and additional chopped parsley. Serve hot with your choice of side dishes, such as steamed vegetables or pasta, and enjoy this delightful French-inspired dish with a glass of Viognier wine.

Notes

Viognier
Chicken Cordon Bleu Casserole

MAIN COURSE

Viognier Wine Chicken Cordon Bleu Casserole is a comforting twist on the classic French dish. It combines layers of tender chicken, smoky ham, Swiss cheese, and a creamy Viognier wine sauce, all baked to golden perfection. Makes 6 servings.

Ingredients:

- 4 boneless, skinless chicken breasts, cooked and diced
- 8 slices Swiss cheese
- 8 slices deli ham
- 1 cup Viognier wine
- 1 cup heavy cream
- 1 cup chicken broth
- 2 tablespoons Dijon mustard
- 1 teaspoon garlic powder
- 1/2 teaspoon onion powder
- 1/2 teaspoon dried thyme
- Salt and black pepper to taste
- 2 cups panko breadcrumbs
- 1/4 cup unsalted butter, melted
- Chopped fresh parsley for garnish (optional)

INSTRUCTIONS:

1. Preheat the Oven:
Preheat your oven to 375°F (190°C). Grease a 9x13-inch baking dish.

2. Layer the Chicken:
Arrange the diced cooked chicken in an even layer in the bottom of the prepared baking dish.

3. Add Ham and Cheese:
Layer the Swiss cheese slices over the chicken, followed by the slices of deli ham.

4. Make the Viognier Wine Sauce:
In a saucepan, combine the Viognier wine, heavy cream, chicken broth, Dijon mustard, garlic powder, onion powder, dried thyme, salt, and black pepper. Heat the mixture over medium heat, stirring until it's well combined and starts to simmer. Simmer for a few minutes until it thickens slightly.

5. Pour the Sauce:
Pour the Viognier wine sauce evenly over the ham and cheese layers in the baking dish.

6. Prepare the Topping:
In a small bowl, mix together the panko breadcrumbs and melted butter until the breadcrumbs are coated.

7. Top and Bake:
Sprinkle the breadcrumb mixture evenly over the casserole.

8. Bake:
Place the casserole in the preheated oven and bake for about 30-35 minutes, or until the top is golden brown and the casserole is bubbly.

9. Garnish and Serve:
If desired, garnish with chopped fresh parsley before serving. Scoop out portions and serve hot.

NOTES

Viognier Lobster Thermidor
with Béchamel Sauce — MAIN COURSE

Viognier Wine Lobster Thermidor is a luxurious seafood dish where lobster tails are smothered in a creamy Viognier wine sauce then broiled to perfection with Béchamel sauce served on the side. This recipe is a delightful way to elevate lobster to a gourmet level. Makes 2 servings.

Ingredients:

For the Lobster Thermidor:
- 2 lobster tails, split in half lengthwise
- 2 tablespoons unsalted butter
- 2 cloves garlic, minced
- 1/4 cup Viognier wine
- 1/2 cup heavy cream
- 1/2 cup shredded Gruyère cheese
- 2 tablespoons grated Parmesan cheese
- 1 teaspoon Dijon mustard
- 1/2 teaspoon paprika
- Salt and black pepper to taste
- Fresh chives or parsley for garnish (optional)

For the Béchamel Sauce:
- 2 tablespoons unsalted butter
- 2 tablespoons all-purpose flour
- 1 cup whole milk
- Salt and white pepper to taste
- A pinch of nutmeg

INSTRUCTIONS:

1. Preheat the Broiler:
Preheat your broiler to high.

2. Prepare the Lobster Tails:
Place the split lobster tails on a baking sheet, shell side down. Season with a little salt and pepper.

3. Broil the Lobster:
Broil the lobster tails for about 5-7 minutes, or until the meat is opaque and lightly browned.

4. Make the Béchamel Sauce:
In a saucepan, melt 2 tablespoons of butter over medium heat. Stir in the flour to make a roux and cook for about 1-2 minutes until it's lightly golden. Gradually whisk in the whole milk and cook, stirring constantly, until the sauce thickens. Season with salt, white pepper, and a pinch of nutmeg. Remove from heat.

5. Prepare the Viognier Wine Sauce:
In a separate saucepan, melt 2 tablespoons of butter over medium heat. Add the minced garlic and sauté for about 1 minute until fragrant. Pour in the Viognier wine and let it simmer for a couple of minutes to reduce slightly. Reduce heat to low, then add the heavy cream, Gruyère cheese, Parmesan cheese, Dijon mustard, and paprika. Stir until the cheeses are melted, and the sauce is creamy. Season with salt and black pepper to taste.

6. Combine Sauces:
Carefully remove the lobster tails from the broiler. Spoon the Viognier wine sauce evenly over the lobster meat.

7. Broil Again:
Return the lobster tails to the broiler and broil for an additional 2-3 minutes, or until the sauce is bubbly and lightly browned.

8. Garnish and Serve:
Garnish with fresh chives or parsley, if desired. Serve with Béchamel Sauce immediately while it's hot and bubbling.

NOTES

Viognier Apple Cranberry Galette

DESSERT

Viognier Wine Apple Cranberry Galette is a rustic and delightful dessert that combines the sweet-tart flavors of apples and cranberries with a hint of Viognier wine. This galette is encased in a buttery, flaky crust and makes for a perfect ending to any meal. Makes 6-8 servings.

Ingredients:

For the Galette Dough:
- 1 1/4 cups all-purpose flour
- 1/4 teaspoon salt
- 1/2 cup unsalted butter, cold and cubed
- 1/4 cup ice water

For the Filling:
- 3-4 medium-sized apples, peeled, cored, and thinly sliced
- 1 cup fresh or frozen cranberries
- 1/2 cup granulated sugar
- 1/4 cup Viognier wine
- 1 tablespoon cornstarch
- 1/2 teaspoon ground cinnamon
- 1/4 teaspoon ground nutmeg
- Zest of 1 lemon
- 1 egg (for egg wash)
- 1 tablespoon coarse sugar (for sprinkling)
- Vanilla ice cream or whipped cream for serving (optional)

Instructions:

1. Prepare the Galette Dough:
In a food processor, combine the flour and salt. Add the cold, cubed butter and pulse until the mixture resembles coarse crumbs. Slowly drizzle in the ice water and pulse just until the dough comes together. Shape the dough into a disk, wrap it in plastic wrap, and refrigerate for at least 30 minutes.

2. Preheat the Oven:
Preheat your oven to 375°F (190°C).

3. Make the Filling:
In a large mixing bowl, combine the thinly sliced apples, cranberries, granulated sugar, Viognier wine, cornstarch, ground cinnamon, ground nutmeg, and lemon zest. Toss the mixture until the fruit is evenly coated.

4. Roll Out the Dough:
On a floured surface, roll out the chilled galette dough into a circle about 12-14 inches in diameter.

5. Assemble the Galette:
Carefully transfer the rolled-out dough to a parchment paper-lined baking sheet. Pile the apple and cranberry mixture in the center of the dough, leaving a border around the edges. Fold the edges of the dough over the filling, creating pleats as you go.

6. Egg Wash:
In a small bowl, beat the egg. Brush the edges of the dough with the beaten egg and sprinkle with coarse sugar.

7. Bake:
Bake the galette in the preheated oven for 35-40 minutes, or until the crust is golden brown, and the filling is bubbly.

8. Cool and Serve:
Allow the galette to cool for a few minutes before slicing. Serve warm, optionally with a scoop of vanilla ice cream or a dollop of whipped cream.

Notes

Viognier Crepes

DESSERT

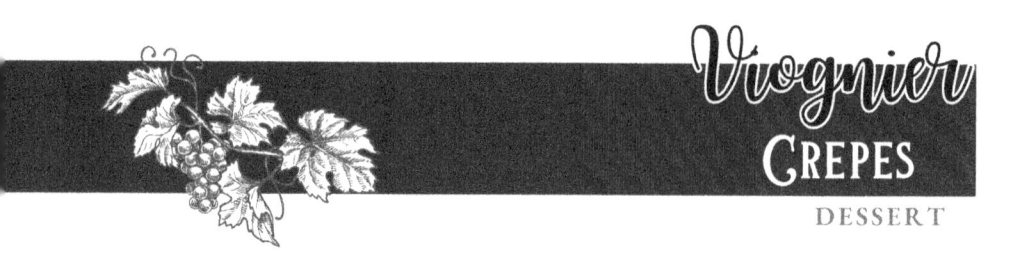

Viognier Wine Crepes are a delicate and elegant dessert option. These thin and lacy crepes are infused with the subtle flavors of Viognier wine and can be filled with a variety of sweet fillings, making them a versatile and delightful treat. Makes approximately 12 crepes, serving 4-6 people.

Ingredients:

For the Viognier Wine Crepes:
- 1 cup all-purpose flour
- 1 1/2 cups whole milk
- 1/2 cup Viognier wine
- 2 large eggs
- 2 tablespoons granulated sugar
- 1/4 teaspoon salt
- 2 tablespoons unsalted butter, melted
- Additional butter or oil for cooking

For Filling and Topping (Optional):
- Fresh berries (strawberries, blueberries, raspberries)
- Whipped cream
- Powdered sugar
- Lemon zest
- Honey
- Nutella or chocolate spread
- Chopped nuts

INSTRUCTIONS:

NOTES

1. Prepare the Crepe Batter:
In a blender, combine the flour, whole milk, Viognier wine, eggs, granulated sugar, salt, and melted butter. Blend until the batter is smooth. You can also whisk these ingredients together in a bowl until well combined.

2. Rest the Batter:
Let the crepe batter rest for at least 30 minutes at room temperature. This allows any bubbles to dissipate and ensures tender crepes.

3. Cook the Crepes:
Heat a non-stick skillet or crepe pan over medium heat and add a small amount of butter or oil to coat the bottom. Pour about 1/4 cup of the crepe batter into the pan, swirling it to cover the bottom evenly. Cook for about 1-2 minutes until the edges start to lift and the crepe is lightly golden. Flip the crepe and cook for an additional 1-2 minutes on the other side. Repeat with the remaining batter, adding more butter or oil as needed. Stack the cooked crepes on a plate, placing a piece of parchment paper or wax paper between each to prevent sticking.

4. Fill and Serve:
Once you've cooked all the crepes, it's time to fill them. You can go sweet or savory. For sweet crepes, consider filling them with fresh berries, a dollop of whipped cream, a dusting of powdered sugar, lemon zest, a drizzle of honey, or Nutella and chopped nuts. For a savory twist, try cheese and herbs, sautéed mushrooms, or smoked salmon with cream cheese.

5. Roll and Enjoy:
Fold or roll the crepes with your chosen fillings, serve them warm.

Tempranillo Wine Notes

~ Food Pairing Suggestions ~

Spanish Cuisine: Tempranillo's Spanish origins make it a natural partner for Spanish dishes like paella, tapas, or chorizo-based dishes.

Grilled Meats: It pairs beautifully with grilled meats, including lamb chops, pork tenderloin, and grilled sausages.

Beef: Tempranillo complements beef dishes, such as beef stew, roast beef, or carne asada.

Mushroom-Based Dishes: Its earthy qualities make it a great match for dishes featuring mushrooms, like mushroom risotto or beef Wellington.

Hard Cheeses: Enjoy it with hard cheeses like Manchego or aged cheddar.

Mexican Cuisine: Tempranillo's versatility allows it to work with Mexican dishes, including enchiladas, mole, and carne guisada.

Tomato-Based Dishes: It pairs well with dishes featuring tomato-based sauces, like spaghetti bolognese or lasagna.

Herb-Seasoned Dishes: Tempranillo's herbal hints complement dishes seasoned with fresh herbs, such as rosemary-infused roasted chicken.

Tapenade and Olives: It pairs beautifully with tapenade and olives, making it a delightful choice for appetizers.

Chocolate Desserts: Its fruity and spicy notes harmonize with chocolate desserts, especially those with dark chocolate and berry components.

PRIMARY FLAVORS
~

Red and Dark Fruits: Tempranillo is known for its flavors of red and dark fruits, including cherry, plum, and sometimes even hints of blackberry.

Spices: It often features subtle spice notes like vanilla, tobacco, and cinnamon.

Earthy Undertones: Some Tempranillo wines showcase earthy qualities such as leather, cedar, or dried leaves.

Herbal Hints: Depending on the region and aging, you may detect herbal nuances like thyme or dill.

TASTE PROFILE
~

Body: Tempranillo typically has a medium to full body, providing a structured and rounded mouthfeel.

Acidity: It often has moderate to high acidity, contributing to its freshness and balance.

Tannins: Tempranillo usually boasts moderate tannins, which add to its structure and aging potential.

Alcohol: It often has a moderate alcohol content, balancing the wine's other components.

Finish: Tempranillo can have a medium to long finish, with lingering fruit and spice notes.

Chapter Eight
Tempranillo

Prepare to embark on a culinary journey that celebrates the essence of Spain and its timeless flavors. At the heart of this adventure lies Tempranillo, a wine that embodies the very soul of Spanish cuisine. More than just a wine, Tempranillo is a storyteller, a bridge between tradition and innovation, and your trusted companion in the kitchen.

In this chapter, we invite you to explore the captivating qualities of Tempranillo, renowned for its vibrant red and dark fruit flavors, subtle spices, and a hint of rustic charm. Beyond its reputation as Spain's signature grape, Tempranillo reveals its culinary prowess, adding depth and character to your dishes.

Tempranillo's versatile flavor profile, marked by cherry and plum notes, a touch of spice, and a whisper of earthiness, makes it the perfect partner for an array of Spanish and international dishes. Whether you're savoring a classic Spanish paella, indulging in the bold flavors of grilled meats, or seeking comfort in a hearty stew, Tempranillo is your culinary confidant.

Join us as we dive into Tempranillo's enchanting qualities through recipes and techniques that celebrate its culinary magic. Throughout these pages, you'll discover how to harness the wine's robust and balanced character, transforming your kitchen into a canvas where flavors mingle and stories are born.

Tempranillo Whiskey Fusion
COCKTAIL

The Tempranillo Whiskey Fusion is a robust and spirited cocktail that combines the earthy richness of Tempranillo wine with the bold character of whiskey. It's a fusion of flavors that's perfect for those who appreciate the depth and warmth of a well-crafted cocktail. Makes one cocktail, easily scalable for multiple servings.

Ingredients:

- 2 oz Tempranillo wine
- 1 1/2 oz whiskey (choose your favorite)
- 1/4 oz honey syrup (mix equal parts honey and warm water)
- 2 dashes aromatic bitters
- Ice cubes
- Orange twist or cherry for garnish (optional)

INSTRUCTIONS:

1. Chill Your Glass:
Place a rocks glass or Old Fashioned glass in the freezer to chill.

2. Prepare the Cocktail:
In a mixing glass filled with ice, combine the Tempranillo wine, whiskey, honey syrup, and aromatic bitters.

3. Stir Well:
Stir the mixture gently for about 15-20 seconds. This chills the ingredients and ensures proper blending.

4. Strain and Serve:
Remove the chilled glass from the freezer and strain the cocktail into it.

5. Garnish:
If desired, garnish your Tempranillo Whiskey Fusion with an orange twist or a maraschino cherry.

6. Enjoy:
Sip and savor this fusion of flavors that marries the earthy depth of Tempranillo wine with the robust charm of whiskey. It's an ideal choice for those who enjoy a spirited and well-balanced cocktail.

NOTES

Tempranillo Singapore Sling
COCKTAIL

The Tempranillo Wine Singapore Sling is a delightful twist on the classic cocktail. With the bold and fruity notes of Tempranillo wine, this drink takes the Singapore Sling to new heights of flavor. Makes 2 servings.

Ingredients:

- 2 oz Tempranillo wine
- 1 oz gin
- 1 oz cherry brandy
- 1/2 oz triple sec
- 1/2 oz Benedictine liqueur
- 4 oz pineapple juice
- 1 oz lime juice
- 1 dash of Angostura bitters
- Maraschino cherries and a slice of pineapple for garnish
- Ice cubes

Instructions:

1. Fill a Shaker:
Fill a cocktail shaker with ice cubes.

2. Add Liquor and Juices:
Pour in the Tempranillo wine, gin, cherry brandy, triple sec, Benedictine liqueur, pineapple juice, and lime juice.

3. Add a Dash of Bitters:
Add a dash of Angostura bitters to the shaker for that classic aromatic touch.

4. Shake It Up:
Secure the lid on the shaker and shake vigorously for about 10-15 seconds. This chills and mixes the ingredients.

5. Strain into Glasses:
Strain the cocktail into two tall glasses filled with ice.

6. Garnish:
Garnish each glass with a maraschino cherry and a slice of pineapple. You can also add a lime wedge if desired.

7. Serve:
Serve your Tempranillo Wine Singapore Sling immediately and enjoy this refreshing and fruity twist on a classic cocktail.

Notes

Tempranillo
Sweet 'n' Tangy Chicken Wings

APPETIZER

Tempranillo Wine Sweet 'n' Tangy Chicken Wings are a mouthwatering blend of crispy chicken wings glazed in a rich, sweet, and tangy Tempranillo wine sauce. These wings are perfect for game day, parties, or any time you're craving a delicious and indulgent appetizer. Makes 4-6 servings.

Ingredients:

- 2 pounds chicken wings, split into drumettes and flats
- Salt and black pepper to taste
- 1/2 cup Tempranillo wine
- 1/4 cup ketchup
- 1/4 cup honey
- 2 tablespoons soy sauce
- 1 tablespoon apple cider vinegar
- 1 teaspoon garlic powder
- 1 teaspoon onion powder
- 1/2 teaspoon smoked paprika
- 2 tablespoons olive oil
- Fresh parsley, chopped, for garnish (optional)
- Sesame seeds, for garnish (optional)

INSTRUCTIONS:

1. Preheat the Oven:
Preheat your oven to 425°F (220°C). Line a baking sheet with parchment paper for easy cleanup.

2. Season the Wings:
Season the chicken wings with salt and black pepper. Arrange them on the prepared baking sheet in a single layer.

3. Bake the Wings:
Bake the wings in the preheated oven for 25-30 minutes or until they are cooked through and crispy, flipping them halfway through the cooking time.

4. Prepare the Tempranillo Sauce:
While the wings are baking, prepare the sauce. In a saucepan, combine the Tempranillo wine, ketchup, honey, soy sauce, apple cider vinegar, garlic powder, onion powder, and smoked paprika. Bring the mixture to a simmer over medium heat and cook for about 10 minutes or until it thickens slightly.

5. Glaze the Wings:
Remove the cooked wings from the oven and transfer them to a large mixing bowl. Pour the Tempranillo wine sauce over the wings and toss them to coat evenly.

6. Broil for Extra Crispiness:
Return the sauced wings to the baking sheet and place them under the broiler for 2-3 minutes until they become caramelized and even crispier. Keep a close eye on them to prevent burning.

7. Serve:
Transfer to a serving platter. Garnish with chopped fresh parsley and sesame seeds if desired. Serve hot.

NOTES

Tempranillo Steak Tartare

APPETIZER

Tempranillo Wine Steak Tartare is an exquisite appetizer that combines the bold flavors of finely minced beef with the rich undertones of Tempranillo wine. It's a sophisticated dish that's perfect for special occasions. Makes 4 servings.

Ingredients:

- 12 ounces high-quality beef tenderloin or sirloin, finely minced
- 1 small shallot, finely chopped
- 2 tablespoons capers, finely chopped
- 2 tablespoons fresh parsley, finely chopped
- 1 tablespoon Dijon mustard
- 2 teaspoons Worcestershire sauce
- 2 teaspoons Tempranillo wine
- 1 egg yolk (optional, for creaminess)
- Salt and black pepper to taste
- Baguette slices or crackers, for serving
- Extra parsley for garnish
- Lemon wedges, for serving

Instructions:

1. Prepare the Beef:
Start by selecting a high-quality cut of beef, like tenderloin or sirloin. Trim any excess fat and finely mince the meat with a sharp knife. Place the minced beef in a mixing bowl.

2. Add the Flavor:
To the minced beef, add the finely chopped shallot, capers, and fresh parsley. These ingredients will provide texture and flavor to the tartare.

3. Season and Mix:
Add the Dijon mustard, Worcestershire sauce, and Tempranillo wine to the bowl. Season with salt and black pepper to taste. Mix all the ingredients together thoroughly.

4. Optional Creaminess:
If you prefer a creamier texture, you can add an egg yolk to the mixture. This is a traditional addition to steak tartare but is entirely optional. Be sure to use fresh, high-quality eggs if you choose to include the yolk.

5. Chill:
Cover the bowl with plastic wrap and refrigerate the steak tartare for at least 30 minutes. Chilling allows the flavors to meld and enhances the dish.

6. Serve:
When ready to serve, shape the tartare into individual portions using a ring mold if desired. Alternatively, you can simply spoon it onto plates. Garnish with extra chopped parsley.

7. Accompaniments:
Serve with slices of baguette or your favorite crackers. Provide lemon wedges on the side for diners to squeeze over their tartare just before enjoying.

Notes

Tempranillo
Espinacas con Garbanzos
"Spinach with Chickpeas" — SIDE DISH

Tempranillo Wine Espinacas con Garbanzos is a delightful Spanish tapas dish that combines the earthy flavors of spinach and chickpeas with the rich undertones of Tempranillo wine. This vegetarian recipe is both nutritious and bursting with savory goodness. Makes 4 servings.

Ingredients:

- 1/4 cup Tempranillo wine
- 2 tablespoons olive oil
- 1 small onion, finely chopped
- 2 cloves garlic, minced
- 1 can (15 ounces) chickpeas, drained and rinsed
- 1 teaspoon ground cumin
- 1/2 teaspoon smoked paprika
- 1/4 teaspoon red pepper flakes (adjust to your heat preference)
- Salt and black pepper to taste
- 10 ounces fresh baby spinach leaves
- 1 tablespoon red wine vinegar
- Lemon wedges for serving (optional)

INSTRUCTIONS:

1. Sauté Onion and Garlic:
In a large skillet, heat the olive oil over medium heat. Add the chopped onion and minced garlic. Sauté for about 2-3 minutes until the onion becomes translucent and fragrant.

2. Add Chickpeas and Spices:
Stir in the drained chickpeas, ground cumin, smoked paprika, red pepper flakes, salt, and black pepper. Cook for another 3-4 minutes, allowing the chickpeas to absorb the flavors.

3. Deglaze with Tempranillo Wine:
Pour the Tempranillo wine into the skillet, using it to deglaze the pan. Scrape up any browned bits from the bottom of the skillet and let the wine simmer for 2-3 minutes until slightly reduced.

4. Wilt the Spinach:
Gradually add the fresh baby spinach to the skillet, a handful at a time. Use tongs to gently toss the spinach with the chickpea mixture until it wilts. Continue adding spinach until it's all incorporated. This should take about 5 minutes.

5. Finish with Red Wine Vinegar:
Drizzle the red wine vinegar over the Espinacas con Garbanzos and give it a final toss. Taste and adjust the seasonings, adding more salt or red pepper flakes if desired.

6. Serve:
Transfer to serving plates. Optionally, serve with lemon wedges for a fresh burst of citrus flavor.

NOTES

Tempranillo Vegetable Tortilla

SIDE DISH

Tempranillo Wine Vegetable Tortilla is a Spanish omelet infused with the deep flavors of Tempranillo wine. Packed with sautéed vegetables and potatoes, it's a hearty and satisfying dish that's perfect for brunch, lunch, or dinner. Makes 8-10 servings.

Ingredients:

- 6 large eggs
- 1/2 cup Tempranillo wine
- 2 cups potatoes, thinly sliced
- 1 onion, thinly sliced
- 1 red bell pepper, thinly sliced
- 1 green bell pepper, thinly sliced
- 1 zucchini, thinly sliced
- 1/2 cup fresh or frozen peas
- 2 cloves garlic, minced
- 1/4 cup olive oil
- Salt and black pepper to taste
- Fresh parsley, chopped, for garnish

Instructions:

1. Prepare the Vegetables:
Heat olive oil in a large skillet over medium-high heat. Add the sliced potatoes and cook for about 5-7 minutes, or until they start to soften. Add the sliced onion and continue cooking for another 3-4 minutes until the onions are translucent.

2. Add Peppers, Zucchini, and Garlic:
Stir in the sliced red and green bell peppers, zucchini, and minced garlic. Cook for an additional 5-7 minutes until the vegetables are tender and slightly caramelized. Add the peas and cook for another 2 minutes. Season with salt and black pepper.

3. Whisk the Eggs and Tempranillo Wine:
In a mixing bowl, whisk the eggs and Tempranillo wine until well combined.

4. Combine Eggs and Vegetables:
Pour the egg and wine mixture over the sautéed vegetables in the skillet. Use a spatula to evenly distribute the vegetables and eggs.

5. Cook the Tortilla:
Reduce the heat to low and cover the skillet. Let the tortilla cook for about 15-20 minutes, or until the edges start to set but the center is slightly runny.

6. Flip and Finish Cooking:
Place a large plate or another skillet of similar size on top of the skillet. Carefully flip the tortilla onto the plate or the other skillet. Slide it back into the original skillet to cook the other side. Continue cooking for an additional 10-15 minutes, or until the tortilla is set and golden brown on both sides.

7. Serve:
Slide onto a serving platter. Garnish with chopped fresh parsley. Allow it to cool slightly before cutting it into wedges. Serve warm or at room temperature.

Notes

Tempranillo Seafood Paella

MAIN COURSE

Tempranillo Wine Seafood Paella is a classic Spanish dish with a twist. This recipe infuses the rich flavors of Tempranillo wine into a savory paella, combining succulent seafood, saffron-infused rice, and a medley of aromatic spices. Makes 4-6 servings.

Ingredients:

- 1 1/2 cups Arborio rice (or other short-grain rice)
- 1/4 cup olive oil
- 1 onion, finely chopped
- 1 red bell pepper, diced
- 1 yellow bell pepper, diced
- 3 cloves garlic, minced
- 1/2 teaspoon smoked paprika
- 1/4 teaspoon saffron threads (soaked in 1/4 cup warm water)
- 1/2 cup Tempranillo wine
- 4 cups chicken or vegetable broth
- 1 cup diced tomatoes (canned or fresh)
- 1 teaspoon salt (adjust to taste)
- 1/2 teaspoon black pepper (adjust to taste)
- 1 1/2 cups assorted seafood (shrimp, mussels, clams, and squid)
- 1/2 cup frozen peas
- Lemon wedges and fresh parsley for garnish

INSTRUCTIONS:

1. Prepare the Saffron Infusion:
In a small bowl, soak the saffron threads in 1/4 cup of warm water. Set aside to infuse.

2. Sear the Seafood:
In a large paella pan or a wide skillet, heat the olive oil over medium-high heat. Add the assorted seafood and sauté for
2-3 minutes until they start to turn opaque. Remove the seafood from the pan and set it aside.

3. Sauté Aromatics:
In the same pan, add the chopped onions and diced bell peppers. Sauté for about 5 minutes until they become soft
and translucent. Add the minced garlic and continue to
sauté for another minute until fragrant.

4. Add Rice and Spices:
Stir in the Arborio rice and smoked paprika. Cook for 2-3 minutes, stirring frequently, until the rice is well-coated with the oil and spices.

5. Deglaze with Tempranillo Wine:
Pour in the Tempranillo wine and stir. Allow it to simmer
for a couple of minutes until it's slightly reduced.

6. Incorporate Saffron and Broth:
Pour the saffron infusion over the rice, along with the diced
tomatoes. Mix well. Gradually add the chicken or vegetable broth, one cup at a time, stirring continuously. Allow the rice to simmer and absorb the liquid before adding more. This process will take about 15-20 minutes until the rice is tender and has a creamy consistency.

7. Add Seafood and Peas:
Return the seared seafood to the pan, along with any juices. Add the frozen peas. Gently fold them into the rice mixture.

8. Season and Finish:
Season the paella with salt and black pepper to taste. Continue to cook for another 5-7 minutes until the seafood is fully cooked, and the peas are tender.

9. Serve:
Garnish with lemon wedges and fresh parsley. Serve it hot, family-style, for a flavorful Spanish feast.

Tempranillo Albóndigas

MAIN COURSE

Tempranillo Wine Albóndigas are Spanish-style meatballs bathed in a rich and flavorful tomato sauce infused with the bold notes of Tempranillo wine. Served with crusty bread or over a bed of rice, they make a satisfying and comforting dish. This recipe yields approximately 20 albóndigas and makes 2-4 servings.

Ingredients:

For the Albóndigas:
- 1 pound ground beef (or a mixture of beef and pork)
- 1/2 cup breadcrumbs
- 1/4 cup milk
- 1/4 cup grated onion
- 2 cloves garlic, minced
- 1 egg
- 1/4 cup fresh parsley, chopped
- Salt and black pepper to taste
- Olive oil for frying

For the Sauce:
- 1 cup Tempranillo wine
- 1 can (14 ounces) crushed tomatoes
- 1 onion, finely chopped
- 2 cloves garlic, minced
- 1 red bell pepper, diced
- 1 teaspoon smoked paprika
- 1/4 teaspoon red pepper flakes (adjust to your heat preference)
- Salt and black pepper to taste
- 2 tablespoons fresh parsley, chopped (for garnish)

Instructions:

1. Prepare the Albóndigas Mixture:
In a mixing bowl, combine the ground beef, breadcrumbs, milk, grated onion, minced garlic, egg, chopped parsley, salt, and black pepper. Mix until all ingredients are well incorporated. Form the mixture into meatballs, about 1 to 1.5 inches in diameter. You should have approximately 20 meatballs.

2. Brown the Albóndigas:
In a large skillet, heat olive oil over medium-high heat. Add the meatballs and brown them on all sides, about 5-7 minutes. Once browned, remove the meatballs from the skillet and set them aside.

3. Prepare the Tempranillo Wine Tomato Sauce:
In the same skillet, add a bit more olive oil if needed. Add the chopped onion and diced red bell pepper. Sauté for about 5 minutes until they soften. Add the minced garlic, smoked paprika, and red pepper flakes. Cook for another minute until fragrant.

4. Deglaze with Tempranillo Wine:
Pour in the Tempranillo wine and stir. Allow it to simmer for a few minutes until it's slightly reduced.

5. Add Crushed Tomatoes:
Add the can of crushed tomatoes to the skillet. Stir well to combine with the wine and aromatic mixture. Season with salt and black pepper to taste.

6. Simmer the Albóndigas:
Return the browned meatballs to the skillet and nestle them into the tomato sauce. Cover and simmer over low heat for about 20-25 minutes, or until the albóndigas are cooked through and the sauce has thickened.

7. Serve:
Sprinkle with fresh parsley and serve them hot, either as an appetizer with toothpicks or as a main course with crusty bread or rice.

Notes

Tempranillo Puchero

MAIN COURSE

Tempranillo Wine Puchero is a hearty Spanish stew featuring a rich broth infused with the bold flavors of Tempranillo wine. This comforting dish combines a variety of meats, vegetables, and legumes for a satisfying and flavorful meal. Makes 6-8 servings.

Ingredients:

For the Stew:
- 1 pound beef chuck, cut into chunks
- 1 pound bone-in pork ribs
- 1 pound Spanish chorizo sausage, sliced
- 1 pound chicken thighs
- 2 cloves garlic, minced
- 2 large potatoes, peeled and diced
- 2 cups butternut squash, peeled and diced
- 2 ears of corn, each cut into thirds
- 2 ripe tomatoes, chopped
- 1 cup chickpeas (canned or cooked from dried)
- 1 cup green beans, trimmed and halved
- 1 small cabbage, cut into wedges
- Salt and black pepper to taste

For the Broth:
- 1/2 cup Tempranillo wine
- 8 cups water
- 1 onion, peeled and halved
- 2 carrots, peeled and halved
- 2 celery stalks, halved
- 2 bay leaves
- 1 teaspoon whole black peppercorns
- Salt to taste

INSTRUCTIONS:

1. Prepare the Broth:
In a large stockpot, combine the Tempranillo wine, water, onion, carrots, celery, bay leaves, whole black peppercorns, and a pinch of salt. Bring to a boil over high heat, then reduce the heat to low, cover, and simmer for about 30 minutes to create a flavorful broth. Strain and discard the solids, retaining the liquid.

2. Brown the Meats:
In a separate skillet, heat a bit of oil over medium-high heat. Brown the beef, pork ribs, chicken thighs, and chorizo slices until they have a nice sear on all sides. Remove them from the skillet and set aside.

3. Start the Stew:
In the same stockpot used for the broth, heat a bit more oil over medium heat. Add the minced garlic and sauté for about 1 minute until fragrant. Return the seared meats to the pot.

4. Add Vegetables and Legumes:
Add the diced potatoes, butternut squash, corn pieces, chopped tomatoes, chickpeas, green beans, and cabbage wedges to the pot. Pour in the prepared Tempranillo broth. Season with salt and black pepper to taste. Stir well to combine.

5. Simmer and Cook:
Bring the mixture to a simmer, then reduce the heat to low. Cover and let it simmer gently for about 1.5 to 2 hours, or until all the meats and vegetables are tender and the flavors have melded together. Stir occasionally.

6. Serve:
Once everything is cooked to perfection, ladle into bowls, making sure to include a variety of meats, vegetables, and legumes in each serving. Serve hot with crusty bread.

NOTES

Tempranillo
Tomato-Herb Grilled Tilapia

MAIN COURSE

Tempranillo Wine Tomato-Herb Grilled Tilapia is a light and flavorful dish that pairs beautifully with a glass of Tempranillo wine. The combination of fresh tomatoes, aromatic herbs, and tender tilapia fillets creates a delightful meal. Makes 4 servings.

Ingredients:

For the Tomato-Herb Topping:
- 2 large tomatoes, diced
- 2 cloves garlic, minced
- 2 tablespoons fresh basil, chopped
- 2 tablespoons fresh parsley, chopped
- 1 tablespoon extra-virgin olive oil
- Salt and black pepper to taste

For the Grilled Tilapia:
- 4 tilapia fillets
- 2 tablespoons extra-virgin olive oil
- 2 tablespoons Tempranillo wine
- 1 lemon, cut into wedges for serving
- Fresh basil leaves for garnish

INSTRUCTIONS:

1. Prepare the Tomato-Herb Topping:
In a bowl, combine the diced tomatoes, minced garlic, chopped basil, chopped parsley, and extra-virgin olive oil. Season with salt and black pepper to taste. This mixture will serve as the flavorful topping for the grilled tilapia.

2. Marinate the Tilapia:
Place the tilapia fillets in a shallow dish. Drizzle them with 2 tablespoons of extra-virgin olive oil and 2 tablespoons of Tempranillo wine. Ensure that the fillets are evenly coated. Let them marinate for about 15 minutes to absorb the flavors.

3. Preheat the Grill:
Preheat your grill to medium-high heat (around 400°F or 200°C). Brush the grill grates with a bit of oil to prevent sticking.

4. Grill the Tilapia:
Place the marinated tilapia fillets on the preheated grill. Grill for approximately 3-4 minutes per side or until the fish flakes easily with a fork and has attractive grill marks.

5. Top with Tomato-Herb Mixture:
While the tilapia is grilling, give the tomato-herb topping a final stir. Once the tilapia is done, transfer it to a serving platter, and generously spoon the tomato-herb mixture over the fillets.

6. Garnish and Serve:
Garnish with fresh basil leaves and lemon wedges. The lemon wedges can be squeezed over the fish just before eating for a burst of citrusy freshness.

NOTES

Tempranillo
Chocolate-Bourbon Pecan Pie

DESSERT

Tempranillo Wine Chocolate-Bourbon Pecan Pie is a luscious dessert that combines the classic flavors of pecan pie with the richness of dark chocolate, the warmth of bourbon, and the subtle undertones of Tempranillo wine. This indulgent pie is perfect for special occasions and gatherings. This recipe yields one 9-inch pie, approximately 8 servings.

INGREDIENTS:

For the Pie Crust:
- 1 1/4 cups all-purpose flour
- 1/2 teaspoon salt
- 1/2 teaspoon granulated sugar
- 1/2 cup (1 stick) cold unsalted butter, cut into small cubes
- 3 to 4 tablespoons ice water

For the Filling:
- 1 cup pecan halves
- 1/2 cup dark chocolate chips
- 3 large eggs
- 1 cup light corn syrup
- 1/4 cup Tempranillo wine
- 2 tablespoons bourbon whiskey
- 1 cup granulated sugar
- 2 tablespoons unsalted butter, melted
- 1 teaspoon pure vanilla extract
- 1/4 teaspoon salt

INSTRUCTIONS:

1. Prepare the Pie Crust:
In a food processor, combine the all-purpose flour, salt, and granulated sugar. Pulse to mix. Add the cold cubed butter and pulse until the mixture resembles coarse crumbs. With the processor running, gradually add ice water until the dough comes together.

2. Chill the Dough:
Turn the dough out onto a clean surface, shape it into a disk, wrap it in plastic wrap, and refrigerate for at least 30 minutes.

3. Preheat the Oven:
Preheat your oven to 350°F (175°C).

4. Roll Out the Dough:
On a lightly floured surface, roll out the chilled pie dough into a 12-inch circle. Carefully transfer it to a 9-inch pie dish. Trim any excess dough hanging over the edges and crimp the edges decoratively.

5. Prepare the Filling:
Scatter the pecan halves and dark chocolate chips evenly over the bottom of the pie crust.

6. Whisk the Filling:
In a large mixing bowl, whisk together the eggs, light corn syrup, Tempranillo wine, bourbon whiskey, granulated sugar, melted butter, pure vanilla extract, and salt until well combined.

7. Pour the Filling:
Gently pour the filling mixture over the pecans and chocolate chips in the pie crust.

8. Bake:
Place the pie on a baking sheet to catch any drips and bake in the preheated oven for 50 to 60 minutes, or until the filling is set. You can cover the edges of the crust with aluminum foil if they start to brown too quickly.

9. Cool and Serve:
Allow the pie to cool completely on a wire rack before serving. Serve slices with a scoop of vanilla ice cream or a dollop of whipped cream, and enjoy!

NOTES

Tempranillo Fudge Brownies

DESSERT

Tempranillo Wine Fudge Brownies are a luxurious twist on classic brownies. These rich, decadent treats are infused with the deep flavors of Tempranillo wine, making them a delightful dessert for wine enthusiasts. This recipe yields approximately 12 brownies.

Ingredients:

- 1/2 cup (1 stick) unsalted butter
- 1 cup granulated sugar
- 2 large eggs
- 1/4 cup Tempranillo wine
- 1 teaspoon pure vanilla extract
- 1/3 cup unsweetened cocoa powder
- 1/2 cup all-purpose flour
- 1/4 teaspoon salt
- 1/4 teaspoon baking powder
- 1/2 cup semisweet chocolate chips

INSTRUCTIONS:

1. Preheat the Oven:
Preheat your oven to 350°F (175°C). Grease and line an 8x8-inch baking pan with parchment paper, leaving an overhang on two sides for easy brownie removal.

2. Melt the Butter:
In a microwave-safe bowl or using a saucepan over low heat, melt the unsalted butter.

3. Combine Wet Ingredients:
In a separate mixing bowl, whisk together the granulated sugar, eggs, Tempranillo wine, and pure vanilla extract until well combined.

4. Add Dry Ingredients:
Sift in the unsweetened cocoa powder, all-purpose flour, salt, and baking powder. Mix until the batter is smooth and no lumps remain.

5. Fold in Chocolate Chips:
Gently fold in the semisweet chocolate chips, reserving a few for topping the brownies.

6. Pour into the Pan:
Pour the brownie batter into the prepared baking pan and spread it evenly. Sprinkle the reserved chocolate chips on top.

7. Bake:
Bake in the preheated oven for 25 to 30 minutes, or until a toothpick inserted into the center comes out with a few moist crumbs. Be careful not to overbake; the brownies should be fudgy.

8. Cool and Slice:
Allow the brownies to cool in the pan for about 10 minutes, then use the parchment paper overhangs to lift them out of the pan. Place them on a wire rack to cool completely.

9. Slice and Enjoy:
Once completely cooled, slice into squares. Serve.

NOTES

MALBEC
Wine Notes

~ Food Pairing Suggestions ~

Grilled Meats: Malbec's bold flavors and tannic structure make it an ideal companion for grilled meats, including steak, lamb chops, and barbecue dishes.

Burgers: It's a fantastic choice for classic burgers, enhancing the flavors of beef patties.

Mole Sauce: Malbec's dark fruit and spice notes pair wonderfully with mole sauces, a staple of Mexican cuisine.

Hard Cheeses: Enjoy it with hard cheeses like aged cheddar or gouda.

Spicy Dishes: Malbec complements spicy dishes, particularly those with a smoky or spicy element, like chili con carne.

Empanadas: It's a classic pairing with Argentine empanadas, enhancing the flavors of the savory fillings.

Pasta with Red Sauce: Malbec works well with pasta dishes featuring tomato-based sauces, such as spaghetti bolognese.

Chocolate Desserts: Its dark fruit and spice notes harmonize with chocolate desserts, especially those with dark chocolate and berry components.

Roasted Vegetables: Malbec's earthy undertones pair nicely with roasted vegetables, such as eggplant or bell peppers.

Barbecue: It's a natural choice for barbecue dishes, whether you're enjoying ribs, pulled pork, or brisket.

PRIMARY FLAVORS

Dark Fruits: Malbec is celebrated for its dark fruit flavors, including blackberry, plum, and black cherry.

Floral Hints: It often features subtle floral notes, like violets, which add a layer of complexity.

Spices: Some Malbec wines exhibit hints of spices, such as black pepper or cloves.

Earthy Undertones: Depending on the region and winemaking style, you may detect earthy qualities like tobacco or leather.

TASTE PROFILE

Body: Typically, Malbec has a medium to full body, offering a smooth and velvety mouthfeel.

Acidity: Malbec generally has moderate acidity, providing a balanced structure.

Tannins: It often boasts moderate tannins, which contribute to its structure and aging potential.

Alcohol: Malbec can have moderate to high alcohol content, adding warmth to the wine's profile.

Finish: Malbec frequently has a medium to long finish, with lingering dark fruit and spice notes.

Chapter Nine
Malbec

Welcome to a culinary journey infused with the vibrant spirit of Argentina and the robust flavors of Malbec wine. In this chapter, we unlock the secrets of Malbec, a wine that embodies the passion and richness of the South American landscape. Beyond being a beverage, Malbec is a muse for the kitchen, a catalyst for culinary excellence.

Malbec's allure lies in its compelling flavor profile – a symphony of dark fruits, subtle florals, and a hint of spice. It's a wine that adds depth and character to your dishes, a co-conspirator in your culinary adventures.

As we delve into this chapter, you'll discover that Malbec's versatility knows no bounds. Whether you're indulging in the bold flavors of grilled meats, savoring the complexity of a hearty stew, or enjoying the elegance of a chocolate dessert, Malbec is your culinary companion.

Join us as we explore Malbec's captivating qualities through recipes and techniques that celebrate its culinary magic. Throughout these pages, you'll find inspiration on how to harness Malbec's bold and velvety character, transforming your kitchen into a realm where flavors dance and memories are created.

Malbec Brandy Blend

COCKTAIL

The Malbec Brandy Blend is a luxurious and velvety cocktail that marries the bold complexity of Malbec wine with the smooth richness of brandy. It's a blend of flavors that's perfect for those who appreciate the deep and sophisticated side of cocktails. Makes one cocktail, easily scalable for multiple servings.

Ingredients:

- 2 oz Malbec wine
- 1 1/2 oz brandy
- 1/4 oz simple syrup (adjust to taste)
- 1 dash Angostura bitters
- Ice cubes
- Orange peel or a grape for garnish (optional)

Instructions:

1. Chill Your Glass:
Place a stemmed wine glass or brandy snifter in the freezer to chill.

2. Prepare the Cocktail:
In a mixing glass filled with ice, combine the Malbec wine, brandy, simple syrup, and a dash of Angostura bitters.

3. Stir Well:
Stir the mixture gently for about 15-20 seconds. This chills the ingredients and ensures proper blending.

4. Strain and Serve:
Remove the chilled glass from the freezer and strain the cocktail into it.

5. Garnish:
If desired, garnish your Malbec Brandy Blend with a strip of orange peel or a single grape.

6. Enjoy:
Sip and savor this luxurious blend of flavors that marries the robust complexity of Malbec wine with the velvety charm of brandy. It's an ideal choice for those who enjoy a refined and sophisticated cocktail.

Notes

Malbec Cognac Fusion
COCKTAIL

The Malbec Cognac Fusion is a luxurious cocktail that melds the deep, fruity richness of Malbec wine with the rich complexity of Cognac. It's a sophisticated and warming concoction for those who appreciate the finer things in life. Makes one cocktail, easily scalable for multiple servings.

Ingredients:

- 2 oz Malbec wine
- 1 oz Cognac
- 1/2 oz honey syrup (made by mixing equal parts honey and hot water)
- 1 dash Angostura bitters
- Orange twist or a cherry for garnish (optional)
- Ice cubes

INSTRUCTIONS:

1. Chill Your Glass:
Place a stemmed wine glass or rocks glass in the freezer to chill.

2. Prepare the Cocktail:
In a mixing glass filled with ice, combine the Malbec wine, Cognac, honey syrup, and a dash of Angostura bitters.

3. Stir Well:
Stir the mixture gently for about 15-20 seconds. This chills the ingredients and ensures proper blending.

4. Strain and Serve:
Remove the chilled glass from the freezer and strain the cocktail into it.

5. Garnish:
If desired, garnish your Malbec Cognac Fusion with a twist of orange peel or a maraschino cherry.

6. Enjoy:
Sip and savor this luxurious fusion of flavors that marries the fruity depth of Malbec wine with the complex charm of Cognac. It's a cocktail for those who seek the ultimate in sophistication and indulgence.

NOTES

Malbec Shrimp Cocktail

APPETIZER

Malbec Wine Shrimp Cocktail is a luxurious appetizer that combines plump, succulent shrimp with a zesty Malbec wine cocktail sauce. This dish is perfect for impressing guests at your next dinner party or enjoying a taste of elegance on a special occasion. Makes 4 servings.

Ingredients:

For the Shrimp:
- 1 pound large shrimp, peeled and deveined
- Salt and black pepper to taste
- 1 lemon, sliced
- Fresh parsley leaves, for garnish

For the Malbec Wine Cocktail Sauce:
- 1/2 cup Malbec wine
- 1/4 cup ketchup
- 2 tablespoons horseradish sauce
- 1 tablespoon Worcestershire sauce
- 1 teaspoon hot sauce (adjust to your heat preference)
- 1 tablespoon lemon juice
- 1 teaspoon lemon zest
- 1/2 teaspoon smoked paprika
- 1/4 teaspoon celery salt
- 1/4 teaspoon black pepper

INSTRUCTIONS:

1. Prepare the Shrimp:
Fill a large pot with water and add a generous pinch of salt. Bring the water to a boil. Once boiling, add the shrimp and cook for 2-3 minutes or until they turn pink and opaque. Drain the shrimp and transfer them to an ice water bath to stop the cooking process. Once cooled, drain again.

2. Make the Malbec Wine Cocktail Sauce:
In a mixing bowl, combine the Malbec wine, ketchup, horseradish sauce, Worcestershire sauce, hot sauce, lemon juice, lemon zest, smoked paprika, celery salt, and black pepper. Mix well to combine. Taste and adjust the seasonings if needed.

3. Chill the Sauce:
Cover the cocktail sauce and refrigerate for at least 30 minutes to allow the flavors to meld.

4. Assemble the Shrimp Cocktail:
To serve, arrange the cooked and cooled shrimp in individual cocktail glasses or on a serving platter. Place a slice of lemon and a sprig of fresh parsley on top of each shrimp. Serve with the chilled Malbec Wine Cocktail Sauce on the side for dipping.

5. Serve:
Present as an elegant appetizer for your guests to enjoy.

NOTES

Malbec Roasted Marrow Bones

APPETIZER

Elevate your appetizer game with Malbec-Infused Roasted Marrow Bones. These rich and decadent bone marrow halves are seasoned to perfection, roasted until golden and creamy, and served with a flavorful Malbec reduction for an unforgettable culinary experience. Makes 4 servings.

Ingredients:

For the Roasted Marrow Bones:
- 4 large beef marrow bones, split lengthwise
- 2 cloves garlic, minced
- 2 tablespoons fresh parsley, chopped
- Salt and black pepper to taste

For the Malbec Reduction:
- 1 cup Malbec wine
- 1/4 cup beef or veal stock
- 1 shallot, finely chopped
- 1 sprig fresh thyme
- 1 tablespoon unsalted butter
- Salt and black pepper to taste

Instructions:

1. Prepare the Marrow Bones:
Place the marrow bones in a large bowl of cold water. Allow them to soak for 24 hours in the refrigerator, changing the water every 8 hours to remove excess blood. This step helps to remove any impurities and soften the marrow.

2. Preheat the Oven:
Preheat your oven to 450°F (230°C).

3. Season and Roast:
Remove the marrow bones from the water and pat them dry with paper towels. Place them in a roasting pan, cut side up. Season each marrow bone half with minced garlic, chopped fresh parsley, salt, and black pepper. Roast in the preheated oven for about 15-20 minutes, or until the marrow becomes soft and starts to pull away from the bone. The tops should be golden brown.

4. Prepare the Malbec Reduction:
While the marrow bones are roasting, prepare the Malbec reduction. In a small saucepan, combine the Malbec wine, beef or veal stock, finely chopped shallot, and fresh thyme sprig. Bring the mixture to a simmer over medium-high heat.

5. Simmer and Reduce:
Allow the mixture to simmer and reduce by half, which may take about 15-20 minutes. Stir occasionally to prevent sticking.

6. Add Butter:
Once the reduction has thickened, remove it from the heat. Discard the thyme sprig and stir in the unsalted butter. Season with salt and black pepper to taste.

7. Serve:
Remove the roasted marrow bones from the oven. Carefully place them on a serving platter. Drizzle the warm Malbec reduction generously over the marrow bones. Serve with crusty bread or toast.

Notes

Malbec Loaded Mashed Potatoes

SIDE DISH

Elevate your mashed potatoes to a new level of richness and flavor with these Malbec-Infused Loaded Mashed Potatoes. Creamy mashed potatoes are infused with the deep, robust taste of Malbec wine, then topped with a medley of delicious toppings. Makes 6 servings.

Ingredients:

For the Malbec-Infused Mashed Potatoes:
- 2 pounds russet potatoes, peeled and cubed
- 1/2 cup Malbec wine
- 1/2 cup whole milk
- 4 tablespoons unsalted butter
- Salt and pepper to taste

For the Toppings:
- 1 cup shredded sharp cheddar cheese
- 1/2 cup sour cream
- 4 slices of bacon, cooked until crispy and crumbled
- 2 green onions, finely chopped
- Fresh parsley, chopped (for garnish)
- Salt and pepper to taste

INSTRUCTIONS:

1. Boil the Potatoes:
Place the peeled and cubed potatoes in a large pot of salted water. Bring to a boil, then reduce the heat to simmer. Cook until the potatoes are fork-tender, usually about 15-20 minutes.

2. Drain and Mash:
Drain the cooked potatoes and return them to the pot. Mash them using a potato masher or a ricer until they're smooth and free of lumps.

3. Infuse with Malbec:
In a small saucepan, heat the Malbec wine over low heat until it's warmed but not boiling. Pour the warm wine into the mashed potatoes and stir to combine. The potatoes will absorb the wine, creating a delightful flavor.

4. Add Butter and Milk:
Add the butter and whole milk to the mashed potatoes. Continue to mash and mix until the butter is melted, and the potatoes are creamy. Season with salt and pepper to taste.

5. Load 'Em Up:
Transfer to a serving dish. Top them with shredded cheddar cheese, sour cream, crumbled bacon, chopped green onions, and a sprinkle of fresh parsley. Add more salt and pepper if desired.

6. Serve:
These loaded mashed potatoes are ready to be served as a scrumptious side dish.

NOTES

Malbec Stuffed Peppers
with Wild Rice & Mushrooms

SIDE DISH

These Malbec-Infused Wild Rice and Mushroom Stuffed Peppers are a hearty and flavorful vegetarian dish. Bell peppers are filled with a savory mixture of wild rice, mushrooms, onions, and Malbec wine, creating a symphony of delicious flavors. Makes 4 servings.

Ingredients:

- 4 large bell peppers, any color
- 1 cup wild rice, cooked according to package instructions
- 2 tablespoons olive oil
- 1 onion, finely chopped
- 2 cloves garlic, minced
- 8 ounces cremini or button mushrooms, finely chopped
- 1/2 cup Malbec wine
- 1 teaspoon dried thyme
- Salt and black pepper to taste
- 1 cup shredded Gruyère cheese (or any preferred cheese)
- Fresh parsley, chopped (for garnish)

INSTRUCTIONS:

1. Prepare the Bell Peppers:
Preheat your oven to 350°F (175°C). Cut the tops off the bell peppers and remove the seeds and membranes from the inside. Set them aside.

2. Cook the Wild Rice:
Cook the wild rice according to the package instructions until it's tender and the grains have split. This usually takes about 45-60 minutes. Drain any excess liquid and set the cooked rice aside.

3. Sauté the Vegetables:
In a large skillet, heat the olive oil over medium heat. Add the chopped onion and garlic, and sauté until they become translucent, about 3-4 minutes.

4. Add Mushrooms and Malbec:
Add the chopped mushrooms to the skillet and cook for another 5-7 minutes, or until they release their moisture and begin to brown. Pour in the Malbec wine and dried thyme. Cook for an additional 5 minutes, allowing the wine to reduce. Season with salt and black pepper to taste.

5. Combine with Wild Rice:
Remove the skillet from heat and mix the cooked wild rice into the mushroom mixture. Ensure everything is well combined.

6. Stuff the Peppers:
Stuff each bell pepper with the wild rice and mushroom mixture, pressing down gently to pack the filling. Top each pepper with shredded Gruyère cheese.

7. Bake:
Place the stuffed peppers in a baking dish and cover with aluminum foil. Bake in the preheated oven for 30-35 minutes, or until the peppers are tender.

8. Serve:
Carefully remove the stuffed peppers from the oven, garnish with chopped fresh parsley, and serve hot.

NOTES

Malbec
Grilled Portobello Mushroom Steaks

MAIN COURSE

Elevate your vegetarian grilling game with Malbec-Infused Grilled Portobello Mushroom Steaks. These hearty mushrooms are marinated in a rich Malbec wine sauce, grilled to perfection, and served with a flavorful reduction, creating a satisfying and savory dish. Makes 4 servings.

Ingredients:

For the Malbec Marinade:
- 1 cup Malbec wine
- 1/4 cup balsamic vinegar
- 2 cloves garlic, minced
- 2 tablespoons fresh rosemary, chopped
- 2 tablespoons olive oil
- Salt and black pepper to taste

For the Grilled Portobello Mushroom Steaks:
- 4 large Portobello mushroom caps, cleaned and stems removed
- 2 tablespoons olive oil
- Salt and black pepper to taste

For the Malbec Reduction:
- 1 cup Malbec wine
- 1/4 cup vegetable broth
- 1 shallot, finely chopped
- 1 sprig fresh thyme
- 1 tablespoon unsalted butter
- Salt and black pepper to taste

INSTRUCTIONS:

1. Prepare the Malbec Marinade:
In a mixing bowl, combine the Malbec wine, balsamic vinegar, minced garlic, chopped fresh rosemary, olive oil, salt, and black pepper. Whisk the ingredients together to create the marinade.

2. Marinate the Mushrooms:
Place the cleaned Portobello mushroom caps in a large, shallow dish. Pour the Malbec marinade over the mushrooms, ensuring they are well-coated. Cover and refrigerate for at least 30 minutes, allowing the mushrooms to soak up the flavors.

3. Preheat the Grill:
Preheat your grill to medium-high heat (around 400°F or 200°C).

4. Grill the Mushrooms:
Remove the marinated mushrooms from the dish, letting any excess marinade drip off. Brush the mushroom caps with olive oil and season with salt and black pepper. Place them on the preheated grill, gill side down. Grill for approximately 4-5 minutes per side, or until the mushrooms are tender and have grill marks.

5. Prepare the Malbec Reduction:
While the mushrooms are grilling, prepare the Malbec reduction. In a small saucepan, combine the Malbec wine, vegetable broth, finely chopped shallot, and fresh thyme sprig. Bring the mixture to a simmer over medium-high heat.

6. Simmer and Reduce:
Allow the mixture to simmer and reduce by half, which may take about 15-20 minutes. Stir occasionally to prevent sticking.

7. Add Butter:
Once the reduction has thickened, remove it from the heat. Discard the thyme sprig and stir in the unsalted butter. Season with salt and black pepper to taste.

8. Serve:
Place the grilled Portobello mushroom steaks on a serving platter. Drizzle the warm Malbec reduction generously over the mushrooms.

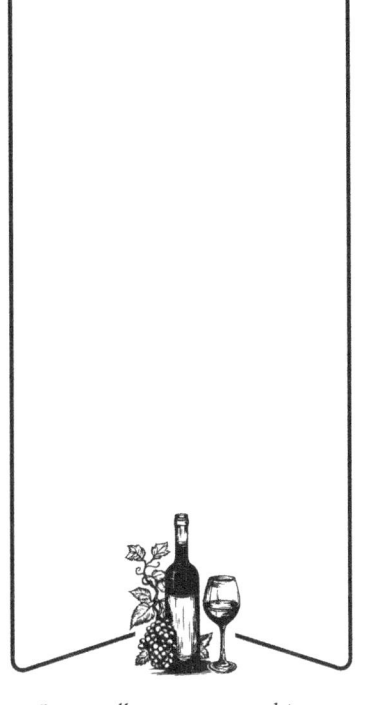

NOTES

Malbec Carne Asada

MAIN COURSE

Malbec Wine Carne Asada with Grilled Onions is a mouthwatering dish that combines tender, marinated beef with the rich flavors of Malbec wine. Grilled onions add a sweet and smoky dimension to this classic Latin American favorite. Makes 4 servings.

Ingredients:

For the Carne Asada Marinade:
- 2 pounds flank or skirt steak
- 1 cup Malbec wine
- 3 cloves garlic, minced
- 1/4 cup fresh lime juice
- 1/4 cup fresh orange juice
- 2 teaspoons ground cumin
- 2 teaspoons chili powder
- 1 teaspoon paprika
- Salt and black pepper to taste

For the Grilled Onions:
- 2 large onions, peeled and sliced into thick rings
- 2 tablespoons olive oil
- Salt and black pepper to taste

INSTRUCTIONS:

1. Prepare the Carne Asada Marinade:
In a bowl, combine the Malbec wine, minced garlic, fresh lime juice, fresh orange juice, ground cumin, chili powder, paprika, salt, and black pepper. Mix well to create a flavorful marinade.

2. Marinate the Steak:
Place the flank or skirt steak in a shallow dish or resealable plastic bag. Pour the marinade over the steak, ensuring it's evenly coated. Seal the bag or cover the dish and refrigerate for at least 2 hours, or overnight for best results. Allow the steak to marinate in the Malbec wine mixture, absorbing all the flavors.

3. Preheat the Grill:
Preheat your grill to medium-high heat.

4. Grill the Steak:
Remove the steak from the marinade and discard the marinade. Place the steak on the preheated grill and grill for approximately 4-6 minutes per side, depending on your desired level of doneness. For medium-rare, aim for an internal temperature of about 130°F (54°C).

5. Grill the Onions:
While the steak is grilling, toss the sliced onions with olive oil, salt, and black pepper. Grill the onions alongside the steak until they become tender and develop grill marks, about 4-5 minutes per side. Remove the grilled onions from the grill.

6. Rest and Slice:
Allow the grilled steak to rest for a few minutes to retain its juices. Then, slice the steak thinly against the grain to maximize tenderness.

7. Serve:
Arrange the slices on a serving platter, and top them with the grilled onions. This dish pairs wonderfully with traditional sides like warm tortillas, guacamole, and salsa.

NOTES

Malbec Grilled Ribeye Steak

MAIN COURSE

Elevate your grilling game with this Grilled Ribeye Steak infused with a luscious Malbec wine reduction. The steak is seasoned to perfection, grilled to your preferred doneness, and then drizzled with a rich wine reduction, resulting in a mouthwatering masterpiece. Makes 2 servings.

Ingredients:

For the Ribeye Steak:
- 2 boneless ribeye steaks, about 1.5 inches thick
- 2 tablespoons olive oil
- 2 cloves garlic, minced
- 1 teaspoon dried rosemary
- 1 teaspoon dried thyme
- Salt and black pepper to taste

For the Malbec Wine Reduction:
- 1 cup Malbec wine
- 1/4 cup beef broth
- 1 shallot, finely chopped
- 1 sprig fresh rosemary
- 1 tablespoon unsalted butter
- Salt and black pepper to taste

INSTRUCTIONS:

1. Prepare the Ribeye Steaks:
In a small bowl, combine the olive oil, minced garlic, dried rosemary, dried thyme, salt, and black pepper. Rub this mixture evenly over both sides of the ribeye steaks. Allow the steaks to marinate at room temperature for about 30 minutes.

2. Preheat the Grill:
Preheat your grill to high heat, aiming for a temperature of around 450°F (230°C).

3. Grill the Steaks:
Place the seasoned ribeye steaks on the hot grill. Grill for approximately 3-4 minutes on each side for medium-rare, or adjust the cooking time to your desired doneness. Use a meat thermometer to check the internal temperature; it should read around 130°F (54°C) for medium-rare.

4. Rest the Steaks:
Remove the steaks from the grill and let them rest on a cutting board, loosely covered with aluminum foil, for about 5 minutes. This resting period allows the juices to redistribute, ensuring a juicy and flavorful steak.

5. Prepare the Malbec Wine Reduction:
While the steaks are resting, prepare the wine reduction. In a small saucepan, combine the Malbec wine, beef broth, finely chopped shallot, and fresh rosemary sprig. Bring the mixture to a simmer over medium-high heat.

6. Simmer and Reduce:
Allow the mixture to simmer and reduce by half, which may take about 10-15 minutes. Stir occasionally to prevent sticking.

7. Add Butter:
Once the reduction has thickened, remove it from the heat. Discard the rosemary sprig and stir in the unsalted butter. Season with salt and black pepper to taste.

8. Slice and Serve:
Slice the grilled ribeye steaks against the grain into thin strips. Plate them and drizzle generously with the Malbec wine reduction.

NOTES

Malbec Bison Burger

with Garlic & Jalapeno

MAIN COURSE

Elevate your burger game with these Malbec-Infused Garlic & Jalapeno Bison Burgers. Juicy bison meat is mixed with bold flavors like garlic and jalapeno, then infused with Malbec wine for a truly exceptional burger experience. Makes 4 mouthwatering bison burgers.

Ingredients:

For the Malbec Marinade:
- 1/2 cup Malbec wine
- 2 cloves garlic, minced
- 1 jalapeno pepper, finely chopped (seeds removed for less heat)
- 2 tablespoons Worcestershire sauce
- Salt and black pepper to taste

For the Bison Burgers:
- 1 pound ground bison meat
- 2 cloves garlic, minced
- 1 jalapeno pepper, finely chopped (seeds removed for less heat)
- 1/4 cup breadcrumbs
- 1/4 cup grated Parmesan cheese
- Salt and black pepper to taste
- 4 burger buns, toasted
- Lettuce, tomato, onion, and other desired toppings

INSTRUCTIONS:

1. Prepare the Malbec Marinade:
In a mixing bowl, combine the Malbec wine, minced garlic, finely chopped jalapeno, Worcestershire sauce, salt, and black pepper. Stir well to create the marinade.

2. Marinate the Bison:
Place the ground bison meat in a separate bowl. Add the minced garlic, chopped jalapeno, breadcrumbs, grated Parmesan cheese, salt, and black pepper. Pour in about half of the Malbec marinade (reserve the rest for basting and serving). Gently mix all the ingredients until well combined. Be careful not to overwork the meat.

3. Form the Burger Patties:
Divide the bison mixture into 4 equal portions. Shape each portion into a burger patty, ensuring they are even in thickness to ensure even cooking.

4. Preheat the Grill:
Preheat your grill to medium-high heat (about 400°F or 200°C). Brush the grill grates with oil to prevent sticking.

5. Grill the Bison Burgers:
Place the bison burgers on the preheated grill. Cook for approximately 4-5 minutes on each side for medium-rare, or longer if desired. During grilling, baste the burgers with the reserved Malbec marinade for an added burst of flavor.

6. Toast the Burger Buns:
While the burgers are cooking, lightly toast the burger buns on the grill until they are golden brown.

7. Assemble the Burgers:
Once the burgers are done to your preferred level of doneness, remove them from the grill. Assemble the burgers by placing a lettuce leaf, a bison patty, tomato slices, onion rings, or any desired toppings on the toasted buns.

8. Serve:
Serve hot, alongside your favorite side dishes or a glass of Malbec wine.

NOTES

Malbec Dark Chocolate Truffles

DESSERT

These Malbec-Infused Dark Chocolate Truffles are the epitome of indulgence. Rich, smooth, and decadent, they combine the bold flavors of Malbec wine with the deep, bittersweet notes of dark chocolate, creating a luxurious treat. This recipe yields approximately 20 truffles, making it ideal for sharing or gifting.

Ingredients:

- 8 ounces (about 1 1/3 cups) high-quality dark chocolate, finely chopped
- 1/2 cup heavy cream
- 1/4 cup Malbec wine
- 2 tablespoons unsalted butter, softened
- Cocoa powder, powdered sugar, crushed nuts, or cocoa nibs (for coating)

INSTRUCTIONS:

1. Prepare the Chocolate:
Place the finely chopped dark chocolate in a heatproof bowl.

2. Heat the Cream and Wine:
In a small saucepan, heat the heavy cream and Malbec wine over medium heat. Bring it just to a simmer, then remove it from the heat immediately.

3. Pour Over Chocolate:
Pour the hot cream-wine mixture over the chopped chocolate. Let it sit for a minute to allow the chocolate to melt.

4. Whisk Smooth:
After a minute, gently whisk the chocolate and cream together until you have a smooth, glossy ganache.

5. Incorporate Butter:
Add the softened butter to the ganache and continue to whisk until it's fully incorporated.

6. Chill:
Cover the bowl with plastic wrap and refrigerate the mixture for about 2-3 hours, or until it becomes firm enough to handle.

7. Shape the Truffles:
Once the mixture is chilled and firm, use a spoon or a melon baller to scoop out portions of the ganache. Roll each portion into a small, bite-sized ball and place it on a parchment paper-lined tray.

8. Coat:
Roll the truffles in your choice of coatings. Cocoa powder, powdered sugar, crushed nuts, or cocoa nibs work well. Place the coated truffles back on the parchment paper.

9. Chill Again:
Chill the truffles for another 30 minutes to set.

10. Serve or Gift:
Arrange them on a beautiful platter for serving or package them in an elegant box for gifting.

Malbec
Double Dark Chocolate Cookies

DESSERT

Up your cookie game with these Malbec-Infused Double Dark Chocolate Cookies. These indulgent cookies are rich, chewy, and packed with intense cocoa flavor, enhanced by the addition of Malbec wine for a sophisticated twist. This recipe makes approximately 18 large cookies or 36 smaller cookies, perfect for sharing or indulging yourself.

Ingredients:

- 1 cup all-purpose flour
- 1/2 cup unsweetened cocoa powder
- 1/2 teaspoon baking soda
- 1/4 teaspoon salt
- 1/2 cup unsalted butter, softened
- 1/2 cup granulated sugar
- 1/2 cup brown sugar, packed
- 1 large egg
- 1 teaspoon pure vanilla extract
- 1/4 cup Malbec wine
- 1 cup dark chocolate chips
- 1/2 cup semi-sweet chocolate chips

INSTRUCTIONS:

1. Preheat Oven:
Preheat your oven to 350°F (175°C) and line a baking sheet with parchment paper.

2. Sift Dry Ingredients:
In a medium-sized bowl, sift together the flour, cocoa powder, baking soda, and salt. Set this dry mixture aside.

3. Cream Butter and Sugars:
In a separate large mixing bowl, cream together the softened butter, granulated sugar, and brown sugar until the mixture is light and fluffy, which should take about 2-3 minutes.

4. Add Egg and Vanilla:
Beat in the egg and vanilla extract until well combined.

5. Incorporate Malbec Wine:
Gradually add the Malbec wine to the wet mixture, mixing until fully incorporated. The wine will give the dough a lovely purple hue.

6. Combine Wet and Dry Mixtures:
Slowly add the dry mixture to the wet mixture, mixing until just combined. Be careful not to overmix.

7. Add Chocolate Chips:
Gently fold in the dark chocolate chips and semi-sweet chocolate chips until evenly distributed throughout the dough.

8. Scoop and Bake:
Using a cookie scoop or spoon, drop rounds of dough onto the prepared baking sheet, leaving enough space between each for the cookies to spread.

9. Bake Cookies:
Bake in the preheated oven for 10-12 minutes for smaller cookies or 12-14 minutes for larger ones. The cookies should be set around the edges but slightly soft in the center.

10. Cool and Enjoy:
Remove the cookies from the oven and let them cool on the baking sheet for a few minutes before transferring them to a wire rack to cool completely.

NOTES

Chapter Ten
Other Varietals

Albariño

PRIMARY FLAVORS

Citrus Notes:
Albariño wines are often characterized by zesty citrus flavors, including lemon, lime, and grapefruit.

Stone Fruit:
You may also detect notes of peach or apricot, contributing to the wine's fruitiness.

Mineral Undertones:
Albariño wines often display mineral qualities, reminiscent of wet stones or sea breeze.

Floral Aromas:
Some Albariños feature floral hints, such as white flowers or blossoms.

Cabernet Franc

PRIMARY FLAVORS

Fruit:
Cabernet Franc often offers vibrant red fruit flavors like red cherry, raspberry, and cranberry, along with blackcurrant and plum notes.

Herbal and Vegetal:
It's known for its unique herbaceous qualities, such as green bell pepper, mint, and sometimes even a hint of tobacco or cigar box.

Spices:
Hints of spices such as black pepper, cinnamon, and clove can add complexity.

Earthy:
Subtle earthy undertones, such as graphite or green olives, can be present.

Grenache

PRIMARY FLAVORS

Red Fruits:
Grenache wines are known for their bright red fruit flavors, including ripe strawberries, raspberries, and red cherries.

Black Fruits:
In some expressions, you may also find hints of black fruit notes like blackberries and plums.

Spices:
Grenache often features subtle spice characteristics, such as white pepper, cinnamon, and licorice.

Herbs:
Earthy and herbal undertones like thyme, lavender, and dried herbs are occasionally present.

Floral:
Some Grenache wines exhibit floral notes, including violets and rose petals.

Petit Verdot

PRIMARY FLAVORS

Dark Fruits:
Petit Verdot is often associated with dark fruit flavors, including blackberry, black cherry, and black plum.

Floral:
Some expressions of Petit Verdot may display floral notes, such as violet and lavender.

Herbs:
Earthy and herbal undertones like green bell pepper, eucalyptus, and thyme are common.

Spices:
It can feature a touch of spice, with elements of black pepper, anise, and licorice.

Tobacco and Leather:
Occasionally, you may detect tobacco leaf and leather aromas, adding complexity.

Chapter Ten
Other Varietals

Petite Sirah

PRIMARY FLAVORS

Dark Fruits:
Petite Sirah is known for its rich and dark fruit flavors, including blackberry, black cherry, and blueberry.

Spices:
It often features notes of spices such as black pepper, clove, and cinnamon.

Earthy and Herbal:
You may detect earthy undertones, along with hints of herbs like thyme and sage.

Chocolate and Coffee:
Some expressions of Petite Sirah exhibit chocolate and coffee notes, adding depth and complexity.

Port/Port Style

PRIMARY FLAVORS

Sweet Red and Black Fruits:
Port wine is known for its rich, sweet red and black fruit flavors, including ripe cherries, blackberries, and plums.

Dried Fruits:
It often features notes of dried fruits, such as raisins, figs, and dates, which contribute to its sweet and complex character.

Nuts:
Some Ports may exhibit nutty flavors, particularly almonds and walnuts.

Chocolate and Cocoa:
Many Ports have chocolate and cocoa notes, adding depth and sweetness.

Rosé

PRIMARY FLAVORS

Red Berries:
Rosé wine is known for its bright and refreshing red berry flavors, including strawberries, raspberries, and red cherries.

Citrus:
It often features notes of citrus fruits, such as grapefruit, orange zest, and lemon, which contribute to its crisp and zesty character.

Floral:
Rosé wines may exhibit floral hints, particularly rose petals and hibiscus.

Mineral:
Some expressions of Rosé may have mineral undertones, which add complexity and a refreshing quality.

Herbs:
You may detect herbal notes, such as thyme and basil, especially in Provence-style Rosés.

Sauvignon Blanc

PRIMARY FLAVORS

Citrus:
Sauvignon Blanc is known for its vibrant and zesty citrus flavors, including grapefruit, lime, and lemon.

Herbs:
It often features herbal notes, such as freshly cut grass, green bell pepper, and basil.

Tropical Fruits:
Some Sauvignon Blanc wines may exhibit tropical fruit characteristics like passion fruit, pineapple, and guava.

Mineral:
Sauvignon Blanc may have mineral undertones, which add a crisp and refreshing quality.

Green Apple and Pear:
You may detect notes of green apple and pear, contributing to its crisp and clean profile.

Albariño Peach Sangria
COCKTAIL

Enjoy the refreshing and fruity flavors of Albariño wine combined with ripe peaches and zesty citrus in this delightful sangria cocktail. Perfect for sipping on warm evenings or entertaining guests. Makes 4-6 servings.

Ingredients:

- 1 bottle (750 ml) Albariño wine
- 1/4 cup peach schnapps
- 2 ripe peaches, sliced
- 1 orange, thinly sliced
- 1 lemon, thinly sliced
- 1/4 cup granulated sugar
- 1/4 cup orange juice
- 1/4 cup lemon juice
- 1 cup club soda or sparkling water
- Ice cubes
- Fresh mint leaves, for garnish

Instructions:

1. In a large pitcher, combine the Albariño wine and peach schnapps.

2. Add the sliced peaches, orange slices, and lemon slices to the pitcher.

3. In a separate bowl, make the sweet citrus mix by combining the granulated sugar, orange juice, and lemon juice. Stir until the sugar dissolves completely.

4. Pour the sweet citrus mix into the pitcher with the wine and fruit.

5. Stir everything together, cover the pitcher, and refrigerate for at least 2 hours (or overnight for a more intense flavor).

6. Just before serving, add the club soda or sparkling water to the pitcher and gently stir to combine.

7. Fill glasses with ice cubes and pour the Albariño Peach Sangria over the ice.

8. Garnish with fresh mint leaves for a burst of aroma and color.

9. Serve.

Notes

Sauvignon Blanc White Sangria

COCKTAIL

This Sauvignon Blanc-based White Sangria is a refreshing and fruity cocktail that combines crisp white wine with citrus and summer fruits. It's the ideal drink for warm gatherings and relaxation. Makes 6-8 servings.

Ingredients:

- 1 bottle (750 ml) Sauvignon Blanc wine
- 1/2 cup triple sec (orange liqueur)
- 1/4 cup brandy
- 1/4 cup granulated sugar
- 1 orange, thinly sliced
- 1 lemon, thinly sliced
- 1 lime, thinly sliced
- 1 green apple, cored and thinly sliced
- 1 cup seedless white grapes, halved
- 1-2 cups club soda or sparkling water (adjust to taste)
- Ice cubes
- Fresh mint leaves (for garnish)

INSTRUCTIONS:

1. In a large pitcher, combine the Sauvignon Blanc wine, triple sec, brandy, and granulated sugar. Stir until the sugar is dissolved.

2. Add the sliced orange, lemon, lime, green apple, and grapes to the pitcher. Mix to combine.

3. Cover the pitcher and refrigerate for at least 2 hours to let the flavors meld. Longer chilling, even overnight, will intensify the flavors.

4. Just before serving, add the club soda or sparkling water to the pitcher and stir gently. Adjust the amount to reach your desired level of effervescence.

5. Fill glasses with ice cubes and pour the Sauvignon Blanc White Sangria over the ice.

6. Garnish with fresh mint leaves for a burst of aroma and color.

7. Serve.

NOTES

GUEST RECIPE

Albariño
Poke Nachos
APPETIZER

Savor the fusion of flavors in this Poke Nachos recipe from Teri Kerns at Ramona Ranch Vineyard & Winery. Crispy wonton triangles cradle marinated Blue Fin Tuna, creamy avocado, and a zesty Sriracha-mayo sauce, creating a delightful appetizer or party snack that's both fresh and indulgent.

Ingredients:

- 1 lb fresh Blue Fin Tuna
- 1/4 cup soy sauce
- 2 jalapeños, chopped
- Juice of 2 limes
- 2 cloves garlic, finely chopped
- 2 tablespoons toasted sesame seeds
- 2 tablespoons olive oil
- Fresh wonton wrappers
- Olive oil, for frying
- 1 avocado, diced
- 1/4 cup mayonnaise
- 2 tablespoons Sriracha sauce

INSTRUCTIONS:

1. Prepare the Tuna:
Slice the fresh Blue Fin Tuna into small cubes. In a bowl, combine the tuna cubes with soy sauce, chopped jalapeños, lime juice, chopped garlic, toasted sesame seeds, and olive oil. Set aside some sesame seeds and jalapeños for garnish. Allow the tuna to marinate for 30 minutes in the refrigerator.

2. Fry the Wonton Wrappers:
While the tuna is marinating, take the fresh wonton wrappers and cut them diagonally into triangles. Heat olive oil in a pan over medium-high heat. Fry the wonton triangles in batches until they are crisp and golden brown. Drain them on paper towels.

3. Assemble the Nachos:
Place the fried wonton triangles on a serving platter. Top each wonton triangle with marinated tuna cubes. Sprinkle the reserved sesame seeds and fresh jalapeño slices (if desired) over the tuna. Add diced avocado on top of the tuna.

4. Prepare the Sriracha Sauce:
In a small bowl, combine the mayonnaise and Sriracha sauce until the mixture reaches a runny consistency.

5. Serve:
Drizzle the homemade Sriracha sauce over the assembled poke nachos. Garnish with additional sesame seeds and jalapeños if desired. Serve immediately and enjoy your delicious Poke Nachos! Pair with Ramona Ranch Albariño to take this dish to the next level.

NOTES

PAIR WITH

Ramona Ranch Winery
Albariño

Sauvignon Blanc
Smoked Salmon & Cucumber

APPETIZER

Elevate your appetizer game with this light and refreshing dish, featuring delicate smoked salmon and crisp cucumber, perfectly paired with a Sauvignon Blanc reduction for a touch of elegance. Makes approximately 20-24 bite-sized appetizers.

Ingredients:

For the Sauvignon Blanc Reduction:
- 1 cup Sauvignon Blanc wine
- 2 tablespoons honey
- 1 teaspoon fresh lemon juice
- 1/2 teaspoon fresh thyme leaves
- A pinch of salt

For the Smoked Salmon & Cucumber Appetizer:
- 8 ounces thinly sliced smoked salmon
- 1 English cucumber
- 1/4 cup fresh dill sprigs
- Freshly ground black pepper, to taste

INSTRUCTIONS:

For the Sauvignon Blanc Reduction:

1. In a small saucepan, combine the Sauvignon Blanc wine, honey, fresh lemon juice, fresh thyme leaves, and a pinch of salt.

2. Place the saucepan over medium heat and bring the mixture to a gentle simmer.

3. Reduce the heat to low and let it simmer for about 15-20 minutes, or until the liquid is reduced by half, and the mixture has thickened to a syrupy consistency.

4. Remove from heat and allow it to cool. The reduction will thicken further as it cools.

For the Smoked Salmon & Cucumber Appetizer:

1. Using a vegetable peeler, create thin, long strips of cucumber. Lay them out flat on paper towels to remove any excess moisture.

2. Lay a strip of smoked salmon on a clean work surface.

3. Place a cucumber strip on top of the salmon and roll it up. Repeat for the remaining salmon and cucumber strips.

4. Secure each roll with a toothpick.

5. Arrange the smoked salmon and cucumber rolls on a serving platter.

6. Drizzle the Sauvignon Blanc reduction over the rolls.

7. Garnish with fresh dill sprigs and a pinch of freshly ground black pepper.

8. Serve immediately, offering a delightful blend of flavors and textures that perfectly complement the Sauvignon Blanc wine reduction.

NOTES

Grenache

Grilled Mushroom Antipasto Salad

SIDE DISH

This delightful antipasto salad showcases the smoky goodness of grilled mushrooms, paired with the robust flavors of Grenache wine, making it a perfect starter or light meal. Makes 4 servings.

Ingredients:

For the Grilled Mushroom Antipasto Salad:
- 1 pound mixed mushrooms (e.g., cremini, shiitake, portobello), cleaned and sliced
- 1/4 cup extra-virgin olive oil
- 1/4 cup Grenache wine
- 2 cloves garlic, minced
- 2 sprigs fresh rosemary, minced
- Salt and black pepper, to taste
- 1/4 cup Kalamata olives, pitted and sliced
- 1/4 cup roasted red bell peppers, sliced
- 1/4 cup marinated artichoke hearts, drained and sliced
- 2 tablespoons capers
- 2 tablespoons fresh parsley, chopped
- 1/4 cup crumbled feta cheese (optional)

For the Grenache Wine Vinaigrette:
- 1/4 cup Grenache wine
- 3 tablespoons extra-virgin olive oil
- 1 tablespoon red wine vinegar
- 1 teaspoon honey
- Salt and black pepper, to taste

INSTRUCTIONS:

For the Grilled Mushroom Antipasto Salad:

1. Preheat your grill to medium-high heat.

2. In a bowl, whisk together the extra-virgin olive oil, Grenache wine, minced garlic, minced rosemary, salt, and black pepper to create the marinade.

3. Toss the sliced mushrooms in the marinade, ensuring they are well coated.

4. Grill the marinated mushrooms for about 5-7 minutes, turning occasionally until they are tender and slightly charred. Remove from the grill and set aside.

5. In a large salad bowl, combine the grilled mushrooms with Kalamata olives, roasted red bell peppers, marinated artichoke hearts, capers, and fresh parsley. If desired, add crumbled feta cheese.

For the Grenache Wine Vinaigrette:

1. In a small bowl, whisk together the Grenache wine, extra-virgin olive oil, red wine vinegar, honey, salt, and black pepper until the vinaigrette is well combined.

To Serve:

1. Drizzle the Grenache Wine Vinaigrette over the Grilled Mushroom Antipasto Salad and toss gently to combine.

NOTES

Sauvignon Blanc Asparagus Salad

with Creamy Lemon Vinaigrette

SIDE DISH

This fresh and vibrant asparagus salad is drizzled with a Sauvignon Blanc-infused creamy lemon vinaigrette, offering a delightful balance of flavors and a touch of elegance to your meal. Makes 4 servings.

Ingredients:

For the Salad:
- 1 bunch of asparagus (about 1 pound)
- 1 tablespoon olive oil
- Salt and black pepper, to taste
- 1/4 cup chopped roasted almonds (for garnish)
- 1/4 cup crumbled feta cheese (for garnish)

For the Creamy Lemon Vinaigrette:
- 1/4 cup Sauvignon Blanc wine
- 2 tablespoons fresh lemon juice
- 1/2 teaspoon Dijon mustard
- 2 tablespoons Greek yogurt
- 1/4 cup extra-virgin olive oil
- 1 teaspoon honey
- Zest of one lemon
- Salt and black pepper, to taste

INSTRUCTIONS:

For the Salad:

1. Preheat your oven to 425°F (220°C).

2. Snap off the tough ends of the asparagus and discard them. Cut the asparagus into 2-inch pieces.

3. Place the asparagus on a baking sheet, drizzle with 1 tablespoon of olive oil, and season with salt and black pepper. Toss to coat.

4. Roast the asparagus in the preheated oven for about 10-12 minutes, or until they are tender yet still slightly crisp. Remove and let them cool.

For the Creamy Lemon Vinaigrette:

1. In a small saucepan, heat the Sauvignon Blanc wine over low heat. Simmer until it's reduced by half, about 5-7 minutes. Let it cool.

2. In a bowl, whisk together the reduced Sauvignon Blanc wine, fresh lemon juice, Dijon mustard, Greek yogurt, extra-virgin olive oil, honey, lemon zest, salt, and black pepper until the vinaigrette is smooth and creamy.

To Assemble:

1. Arrange the roasted asparagus on a serving platter.

2. Drizzle the creamy lemon vinaigrette over the asparagus.

3. Sprinkle with chopped roasted almonds and crumbled feta cheese.

NOTES

Petite Sirah

Cheesy Au Gratin Potatoes and Ham

MAIN COURSE

This comforting and hearty dish combines tender layers of potatoes and ham smothered in a rich and creamy Petit Sirah wine-infused cheese sauce. It's the ultimate comfort food with a touch of sophistication. Makes 4-6 servings.

Ingredients:

For the Cheesy Au Gratin Potatoes and Ham:
- 4 cups russet potatoes, peeled and thinly sliced
- 2 cups cooked ham, diced
- 2 cups shredded sharp cheddar cheese
- 1/2 cup grated Parmesan cheese
- 3 tablespoons unsalted butter
- 3 tablespoons all-purpose flour
- 2 cups whole milk
- 1/2 cup Petite Sirah wine
- 1 teaspoon Dijon mustard
- 1/2 teaspoon garlic powder
- 1/2 teaspoon onion powder
- Salt and black pepper, to taste
- Chopped fresh parsley (for garnish)

INSTRUCTIONS:

For the Cheesy Au Gratin Potatoes and Ham:

1. Preheat your oven to 375°F (190°C). Grease a 9x13-inch baking dish and set it aside.

2. In a large saucepan, melt the butter over medium heat. Add the flour and whisk continuously to create a roux. Cook for 1-2 minutes until it starts to turn a light golden color.

3. Slowly pour in the milk, whisking constantly to avoid lumps. Continue to whisk until the mixture thickens, about 5 minutes.

4. Stir in the Petite Sirah wine, Dijon mustard, garlic powder, onion powder, salt, and black pepper. Simmer for an additional 2-3 minutes, allowing the wine to meld with the sauce.

5. Layer half of the sliced potatoes on the bottom of the prepared baking dish. Top with half of the diced ham and half of the shredded cheddar and Parmesan cheeses.

6. Pour half of the wine-infused cheese sauce over the layers.

7. Repeat the layering process with the remaining potatoes, ham, and cheeses.

8. Pour the rest of the sauce over the top layer.

9. Cover the baking dish with foil and bake for 45 minutes.

10. Remove the foil and bake for an additional 20-25 minutes, or until the top is golden brown, and the potatoes are tender when pierced with a fork.

11. Let the dish cool for a few minutes, garnish with chopped fresh parsley, and serve while it's hot and bubbling.

NOTES

Cabernet Franc Baked Penne

with Prosciutto and Fontina — MAIN COURSE

This indulgent pasta dish combines the richness of Cabernet Franc wine with the savory goodness of prosciutto and creamy Fontina cheese. Baked to perfection, it's comfort food elevated to gourmet status. Makes 4 servings.

Ingredients:

- 12 ounces penne pasta
- 4 ounces prosciutto, thinly sliced and chopped
- 2 tablespoons olive oil
- 1/2 cup Cabernet Franc wine
- 2 cups heavy cream
- 2 cups Fontina cheese, shredded
- 1/2 cup Parmesan cheese, grated
- 1/2 teaspoon dried thyme
- 1/2 teaspoon salt
- 1/4 teaspoon black pepper
- 2 tablespoons fresh parsley, chopped (for garnish)

INSTRUCTIONS:

1. Preheat your oven to 375°F (190°C). Grease a 9x13-inch baking dish and set it aside.

2. In a large pot, bring salted water to a boil. Cook the penne pasta according to the package instructions until al dente. Drain and set aside.

3. In a large skillet, heat the olive oil over medium heat. Add the chopped prosciutto and cook for 2-3 minutes, or until it starts to become crispy. Remove the prosciutto from the skillet and set it aside on a paper towel-lined plate.

4. In the same skillet, pour in the Cabernet Franc wine and simmer for about 5 minutes, or until it reduces by half.

5. Reduce the heat to low and add the heavy cream, Fontina cheese, Parmesan cheese, dried thyme, salt, and black pepper. Stir constantly until the cheese is melted and the sauce is smooth and creamy.

6. Combine the cooked penne and the prosciutto with the wine and cheese sauce. Mix thoroughly.

7. Transfer the mixture into the prepared baking dish, spreading it evenly.

8. Bake in the preheated oven for 20-25 minutes or until the top is golden and bubbly.

9. Remove from the oven and let it cool for a few minutes before serving.

10. Garnish with freshly chopped parsley for a pop of color and freshness.

11. Serve hot and enjoy.

NOTES

Petit Verdot BBQ Pulled Pork

MAIN COURSE

Enjoy tender and flavorful pulled pork infused with the robust and fruity notes of Petit Verdot wine. This slow cooker recipe makes the perfect sandwich or meal centerpiece for any barbecue gathering. Makes 6-8 servings.

Ingredients:

For the Pork:
- 3-4 pounds boneless pork shoulder or pork butt
- Salt and black pepper, to taste
- 1 tablespoon smoked paprika
- 1 teaspoon garlic powder
- 1 teaspoon onion powder
- 1 teaspoon dried oregano
- 1/2 cup Petit Verdot wine
- 1 cup barbecue sauce (your choice of flavor)
- 1/2 cup chicken broth
- 1 onion, sliced
- 4 cloves garlic, minced

For Serving:
- Hamburger buns or rolls
- Coleslaw (optional)

INSTRUCTIONS:

1. In a small bowl, mix together the smoked paprika, garlic powder, onion powder, dried oregano, salt, and black pepper.

2. Rub this spice mixture evenly over the pork shoulder, ensuring it's well coated on all sides.

3. Place the sliced onion and minced garlic in the bottom of your slow cooker.

4. Place the seasoned pork on top of the onions and garlic.

5. Pour in the Petit Verdot wine and chicken broth.

6. Cover the slow cooker and cook on low for 7-8 hours or until the pork is fork-tender and easily pulls apart.

7. Once the pork is cooked, carefully remove it from the slow cooker and transfer it to a large cutting board.

8. Shred the pork using two forks, removing any excess fat as you go.

9. In a large bowl, mix the shredded pork with the barbecue sauce to your desired level of sauciness.

10. Return the sauced pork to the slow cooker and let it simmer on the warm setting for an additional 20-30 minutes to absorb the flavors.

To Serve:

1. Serve on hamburger buns or rolls, with optional coleslaw for a classic combination.

NOTES

Cabernet Franc
Pork Tenderloin
with Fruit Chutney   MAIN COURSE

This exquisite pork tenderloin is coated in a rich Cabernet Franc wine glaze and accompanied by a flavorful fruit chutney, making it an elegant and delectable dish. Makes 4-6 servings.

Ingredients:

For the Pork Tenderloin:
- 2 pork tenderloins (about 1.5 pounds each)
- Salt and black pepper, to taste
- 2 tablespoons olive oil
- 1 cup Cabernet Franc wine
- 1/2 cup brown sugar
- 2 cloves garlic, minced
- 1 teaspoon fresh rosemary, minced

For the Fruit Chutney:
- 1 cup mixed dried fruits (apricots, cranberries, raisins, etc.), chopped
- 1/2 cup Cabernet Franc wine
- 1/4 cup apple cider vinegar
- 1/4 cup brown sugar
- 1/2 teaspoon ground cinnamon
- 1/4 teaspoon ground ginger
- Salt and black pepper, to taste

INSTRUCTIONS:

NOTES

For the Pork Tenderloin:

1. Preheat your oven to 375°F (190°C).

2. Season the pork tenderloins generously with salt and black pepper.

3. In an ovenproof skillet, heat the olive oil over medium-high heat. Add the pork tenderloins and sear them until they are browned on all sides, about 2-3 minutes per side.

4. In a bowl, mix the Cabernet Franc wine, brown sugar, minced garlic, and fresh rosemary. Pour this mixture over the seared pork tenderloins.

5. Transfer the skillet to the preheated oven and roast for 20-25 minutes or until the internal temperature of the pork reaches 145°F (63°C), for medium-rare. Baste the pork with the wine glaze a few times during roasting.

6. Once cooked, remove the pork from the skillet and let it rest for 5-10 minutes before slicing.

For the Fruit Chutney:

1. In a saucepan, combine the mixed dried fruits, Cabernet Franc wine, apple cider vinegar, brown sugar, ground cinnamon, and ground ginger. Season with a pinch of salt and black pepper.

2. Simmer over medium heat for about 10-15 minutes, stirring occasionally, until the chutney thickens and the fruits plump up.

3. Taste the chutney and adjust the seasoning or sweetness as needed. Add more sugar if you prefer it sweeter, or a pinch of salt for balance.

To Serve:

1. Slice the roasted pork tenderloins into medallions and arrange them on a serving platter. Drizzle the Cabernet Franc glaze from the skillet over the pork. Serve with the warm fruit chutney on the side.

Port Wine Dark Chocolate Molten Cupcakes

DESSERT

Satisfy your chocolate cravings with these rich and indulgent dark chocolate molten cupcakes infused with the deep, fruity notes of Ruby Port wine. Each bite reveals a luscious, gooey center that will delight your taste buds. Makes 6 decadent cupcakes.

Ingredients:

For the Dark Chocolate Molten Cupcakes:
- 4 ounces dark chocolate (70% cocoa), chopped
- 1/2 cup unsalted butter
- 1/4 cup Ruby Port wine
- 1/2 cup granulated sugar
- 2 large eggs
- 1/4 cup all-purpose flour
- 1/4 teaspoon salt
- 1 teaspoon pure vanilla extract

For Dusting (optional):
- Powdered sugar
- Fresh raspberries and mint leaves (for garnish)

INSTRUCTIONS:

For the Dark Chocolate Molten Cupcakes:

1. Preheat your oven to 400°F (200°C). Grease and flour six cupcake molds or ramekins.

2. In a microwave-safe bowl, melt the dark chocolate and butter together. Microwave in 20-30 second intervals, stirring each time, until the mixture is smooth and fully combined.

3. Stir in the Ruby Port wine until well incorporated into the chocolate-butter mixture.

4. In a separate bowl, whisk the granulated sugar and eggs together until light and fluffy.

5. Gently fold the chocolate-wine mixture into the sugar-egg mixture.

6. Add the all-purpose flour, salt, and vanilla extract, stirring until just combined.

7. Pour the batter evenly into the prepared cupcake molds or ramekins.

8. Bake in the preheated oven for 10-12 minutes, or until the cupcakes are set around the edges but still soft in the centers.

9. Remove from the oven and let them cool for a few minutes.

To Serve:

1. If desired, dust the top of each Ruby Port Dark Chocolate Molten Cupcake with powdered sugar.

2. Serve your cupcakes warm, with a side of fresh raspberries and mint leaves for a touch of color and flavor.

NOTES

Rosé Raspberry Sorbet

DESSERT

Indulge in the perfect summer treat with this elegant and refreshing raspberry sorbet infused with the delicate flavors of Rosé wine. It's a delightful, fruity dessert to cool off on a warm day. Makes 4-6 servings.

Ingredients:

- 3 cups fresh or frozen raspberries
- 1/2 cup Rosé wine
- 1/2 cup granulated sugar
- 1/4 cup water
- 1 tablespoon fresh lemon juice
- Fresh mint leaves (for garnish)
- Fresh raspberries (for garnish)

INSTRUCTIONS:

1. In a saucepan, combine the Rosé wine, granulated sugar, and water. Heat over medium heat, stirring until the sugar dissolves completely. Remove from heat and let it cool to room temperature.

2. In a blender or food processor, blend the fresh or frozen raspberries until smooth. If using frozen raspberries, allow them to thaw slightly before blending.

3. Strain the raspberry puree through a fine-mesh sieve into a mixing bowl to remove the seeds. Press down with a spoon to extract as much liquid as possible.

4. Add the Rosé wine and sugar syrup mixture, along with the fresh lemon juice, to the strained raspberry puree. Stir well to combine.

5. Transfer the mixture into an ice cream maker and churn according to the manufacturer's instructions until it reaches a sorbet-like consistency. This typically takes 20-25 minutes.

6. If you don't have an ice cream maker, you can pour the mixture into a shallow, freezer-safe container and freeze it. Every 30 minutes, stir the mixture with a fork to break up ice crystals until it reaches the desired sorbet consistency (about 2-3 hours).

7. Once the sorbet has reached the desired consistency, transfer it to an airtight container and freeze for an additional 2 hours or until firm.

8. When ready to serve, scoop the Rosé Wine-Infused Raspberry Sorbet into chilled dessert bowls.

9. Garnish with fresh mint leaves and a few whole raspberries for an extra burst of flavor and color.

NOTES

Ramona Wine Region

The Ramona Valley, located in sunny Southern California, is a region steeped in history and renowned for its unique terroir, which has made it a designated American Viticultural Area (AVA). Its vinous journey began in the late 18th century when Spanish missionaries first introduced grapevines to the area as part of their mission-building efforts. However, it wasn't until the late 19th century that commercial grape growing and winemaking took root.

The designation of Ramona Valley as an AVA came much later, in 2006, marking it as one of the newer AVAs in California. This recognition was a testament to the region's distinctive climate, topography, and soil, all of which contribute to the exceptional grape-growing conditions found here. The valley's vineyards benefit from warm, sun-drenched days and cool evenings, which are ideal for a wide range of grape varieties. Additionally, the unique combination of granite-based soils and elevations ranging from 1,400 to 2,600 feet imparts distinct character and complexity to the wines produced in the region.

Today, Ramona Valley boasts a thriving wine industry, with numerous wineries that produce a diverse array of high-quality wines. Visitors to the area can explore the beautiful vineyards, savor award-winning wines, and experience the rich heritage of this remarkable AVA, making it a must-visit destination for wine enthusiasts seeking a taste of California's wine history and innovation.

Wine Tasting Tips

Exploring the wineries of Ramona Valley on a wine tasting day trip is a fantastic experience. Here are some tips to help you make the most of your excursion:

Plan Ahead:
Research the wineries in the Ramona Valley you want to visit and create an itinerary. Check their operating hours, tasting fees, and if they require reservations. Some wineries may have restrictions or special events, so it's important to plan your trip accordingly.

Respect the Hosts:
Be polite and respectful to winery staff. They are knowledgeable and passionate about their wines and will provide you with a better experience if you treat them kindly.

Ask Questions:
Don't hesitate to ask questions about the wines, winemaking process, and the winery itself. Winemakers and staff are often happy to share their expertise and stories.

Remember that wine tasting is about having fun, discovering new wines, and enjoying the company of friends and fellow wine enthusiasts.

Cheers to a memorable day exploring the wineries of Ramona Valley!

Winery Listings Icon Keys

🏠	Indoor Tasting Room	🧺	Bring a Picnic	🌱	Certified Sustainable
⛱	Outdoor Tasting Patio	🐾	Pets Welcome	🚐	Harvest Hosts
🍇	Vineyard View	👫	Kid Friendly	⛺	Glamping

Ramona Valley Wineries Map

Explore the scenic beauty and exceptional wines of Ramona's vineyards with ease using this detailed handcrafted map.

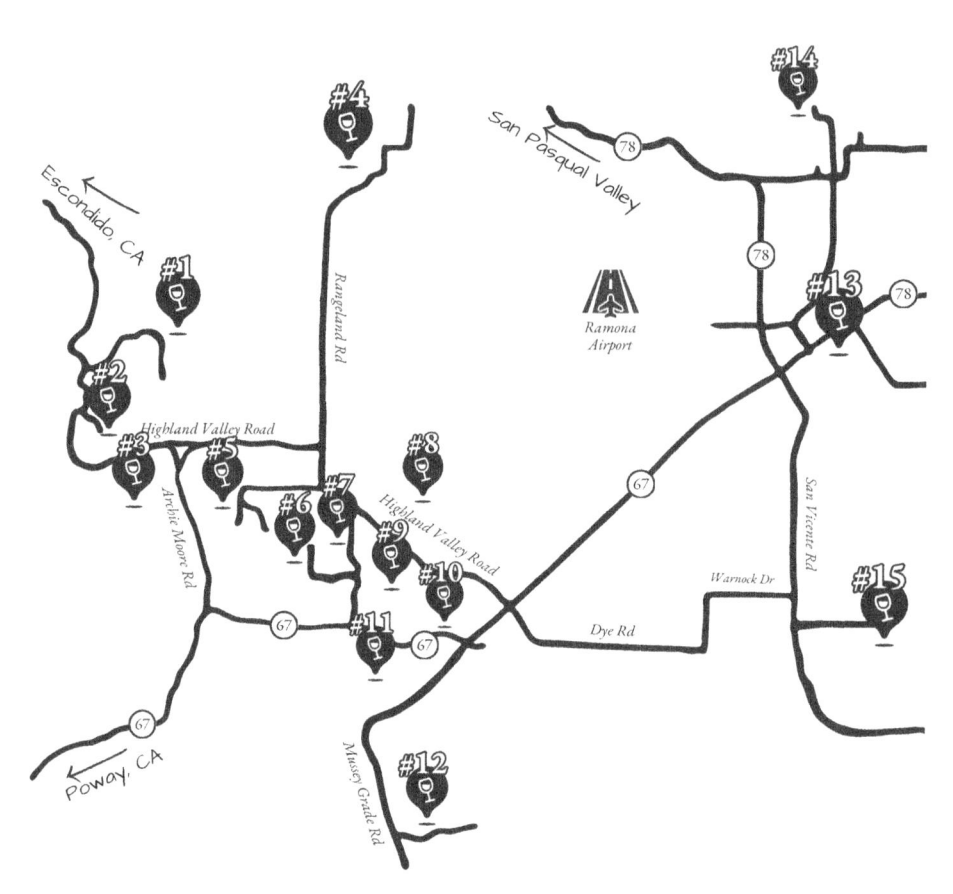

#1 **Sky Valley Cellars**
16729 Sky Valley Dr.

#2 **Sunrise Vineyards**
16620 Highland Valley Rd

#3 **Three Hills Winery**
16805 Highland Valley Rd

#4 **Castelli Family Vineyards**
17872 Oak Grove Road

#5 **Rancho San Martin**
17249 Sundance Dr

#6 **Woof'n Rosé Winery**
17073 Garjan Lane

#7 **Principe di Tricase Winery**
18425 Highland Valley Rd

#8 **Mermaid Valley Vineyard**
18420 Highland Valley Rd

#9 **Cactus Star Vineyard**
17029 Handlebar Rd

#10 **Rashelica Winery**
17948 CA-67

#11 **Schwaesdall Winery**
17677 Rancho De Oro Dr

#12 **Mahogany Mountain Winery**
14905 Mussey Grade Rd

#13 **Pamo Valley Winery**
636 Main Street

#14 **Correcaminos Vineyard**
1941 Lilac Road

#15 **Chuparosa Vineyards**
910 Gem Lane

Ramona Valley Wineries Map

Map not to scale and meant as a guide only.

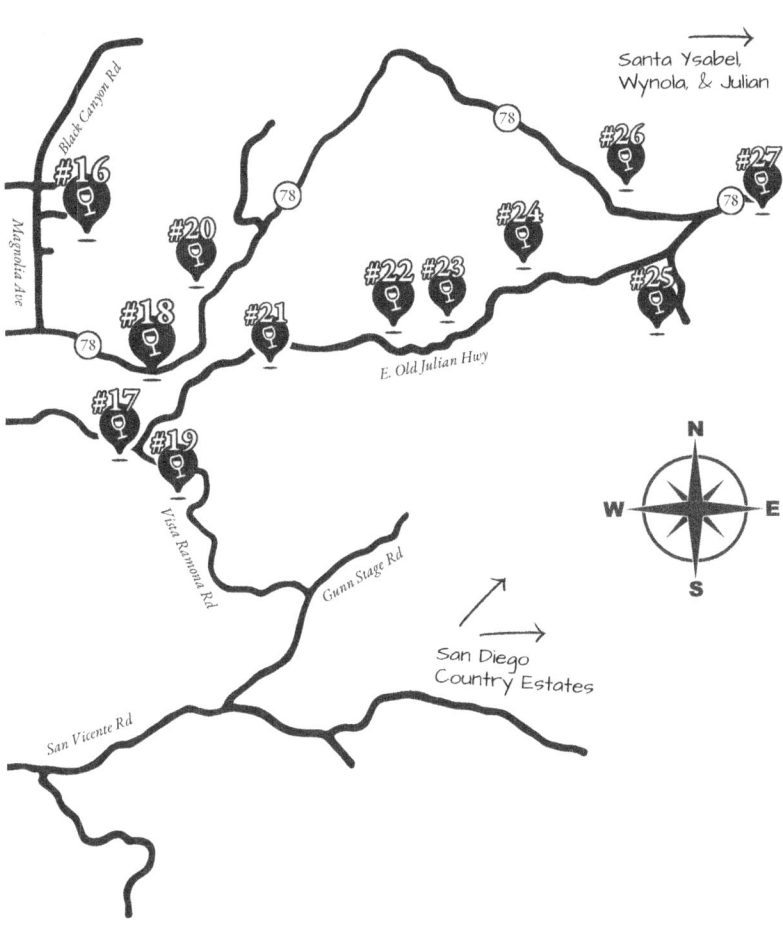

#16 **Barrel 1 Winery**
1007 Magnolia Avenue

#17 **Vina Ramona**
657 East Old Julian Highway

#18 **Hatfield Creek Winery**
1625 Highway 78

#19 **Turtle Rock Ridge**
18351 Woods Hill Lane

#20 **Ramona Ranch Winery**
23578 Highway 78

#21 **Crystal Hill Vineyard**
24067 Old Julian Hwy

#22 **Vineyard Grant James**
25260 Old Julian Hwy

#23 **Old Julian Vineyards**
25352 Old Julian Hwy

#24 **Poppaea Vineyard**
25643 Old Julian Hwy

#25 **Milagro Farm Vineyards**
18750 Littlepage Rd

#26 **Edwards Vineyard & Cellars**
26502 CA-78

#27 **Scenic Valley Ranch Vineyards**
27012 Scenic Valley Rd

Lathom Farm and Vineyard
Opening 2024

~ 269 ~

Barrel 1 Winery

RAMONA, CALIFORNIA

About the Winery

Nestled beneath an ancient volcanic hill in Goose Valley, you'll find the Cassidy Family Estate, the proud home of Barrel 1 Winery. Since planting their first Merlot grapes in 2001, the Cassidy Estate has flourished into one of Ramona's largest vineyards, boasting over 3,000 vines.

Owners Tom and Audrey Cassidy, alongside winemaker Robert Garland, firmly believe in the significance of exceptional fruit as the foundation of great wine. Their dedication to the grapes, nurtured by remarkable soil and weather, yields fruit-forward, full-bodied wines. Volcanic soil, temperature fluctuations, and mature vines create the foundation for the vineyard's exceptional quality, akin to Napa Valley.

Barrel 1 Winery's artisanal approach, from vine to bottle, exclusively features naturally grown estate grapes without the use of fertilizers, pesticides, or fungicides. The Cassidy family proudly opened the Barrel 1 tasting room in April 2015, reminiscent of a Tuscan ranch it offers picturesque vineyard views.

Location & Contact Info

- 1007 Magnolia Avenue, Ramona, CA 92065
- (858) 204-3144
- ajcassidy@barrel1.com
- https://www.barrel1.com

Varieties Available

Cabernet Sauvignon, "Black Widow" Merlot, Tempranillo, Viognier, Tempranillo Rosé, Muscat Canelli

Tasting Room

Saturdays and Sundays 12 PM to 5 PM

*Contact winery to confirm tasting room hours & currently available wines.

Winery

Cactus Star Vineyard at Scaredy Cat Ranch

RAMONA, CALIFORNIA

About the Winery

A boutique winery situated on the western edge of the Ramona Valley AVA. Their journey began in 2001, culminating in the crafting of their inaugural vintage in 2004. As one of Southern California's smallest wineries, they meticulously produce 150-200 cases annually. All their wines are created and bottled on-site by Joe Cullen, winemaker/owner, utilizing all estate-grown grapes.

Cactus Star Vineyard offers award-winning and nationally acclaimed estate wines, labeled as Scaredy Cat Ranch. The grape varietals grown on the ranch are Tempranillo, Cabernet Sauvignon, Petit Verdot and Malbec.

Their winemaking process involves cold soaking, primary fermentation in small macro bins, daily cap punch-downs, followed by pressing and aging in 225-liter French oak barrels. Their tasting patio opens seasonally, typically from Halloween weekend in October to the end of February, or until sold out, offering a glimpse into their world of limited-production, premium wines.

Location & Contact Info

17029 Handlebar Rd, Ramona, CA 92065

(760) 787-0779

info@scaredycatranch.com

https://cactusstarvineyard.com

Varieties Available

Cabernet Sauvignon, Tempranillo, Petit Verdot, Malbec

Tasting Room

Limited days and times, visit their website for details.

*Contact winery to confirm tasting room hours & currently available wines.

Castelli & Pizarro Family Winery

RAMONA, CALIFORNIA

About the Winery

The journey of the winery owners has taken them from a humble hobby to managing 3,000 vines and an underground wine cellar filled with award-winning wines. Guests are invited to experience this transformation at their Italian-style stucco estate, featuring high ceilings and a custom bar surrounded by aging wine barrels.

The story began when Mike Castelli's daughter, Cassie, chose Cordiano Winery for her wedding venue in 2008. Inspired by the Italian owner, Mike started with a few vines, which quickly multiplied to 3,000. Recognizing the need for help, Mike enlisted his son-in-law Nelson to join the venture. Over three dedicated years in the vineyard, they cultivated each vine with care. To prepare for their anticipated wine production, Mike constructed a 1,600 square foot cellar.

Castelli & Pizarro Family Winery is nestled 36 miles east of downtown San Diego in the picturesque Highland Valley just off the Ramona Grassland preserve. Guests are welcomed to their Italian-inspired estate, complete with stucco architecture, lofty ceilings, and a spacious custom bar surrounded by aging wine barrels.

Location & Contact Info

17872 Oak Grove Road, Ramona, CA 92065

(619) 997-5141

info@castellifamilyvineyards.com

castellifamilyvineyards.com

Varieties Available

Viognier, Sangiovese, Tempranillo, Pinot Noir, Syrah, Petit Sirah, Petit Verdot, Cabernet Sauvignon, Cabernet Franc, Chardonnay, Pinot Grigio, & Various Blends

Tasting Room

Saturdays and Sundays 12 PM to 5:30 PM; Also open by appt. At gate push "CALL 191" or 619.997.5141

Contact winery to confirm tasting room hours & currently available wines.

Winery
Chuparosa Vineyards
RAMONA, CALIFORNIA

About the Winery

Chuparosa Vineyards takes pride in its estate-grown, produced, and bottled wines. Their green labeled releases exclusively feature vineyard-designated Ramona Valley grapes, showcasing the meticulous care from harvest to bottle by Chuparosa Vineyards. This winery specializes in crafting 100% estate-grown wines from the heart of the Ramona Valley in San Diego County.

Their tasting room offers a picturesque view of the North Block, home to Sangiovese, Cabernet Franc, and Malbec vines, while the South Block produces their Zinfandel and Albariño varietals. Visitors are warmly welcomed on weekends for wine sales, allowing them to savor the essence of Ramona Valley in every sip. Chuparosa Vineyards embarked on its journey by digging a well in 2002, planting Zinfandel in 2004, and achieving winery licensing in 2006.

They are dedicated to handcrafting small-lot wines that reflect the unique terroir of the Ramona Valley, resulting in exceptional, estate-produced wines.

Location & Contact Info

910 Gem Lane,
Ramona, CA 92065

(760) 788-0059

carolyn@chuparosavineyards.com

http://www.chuparosavineyards.com

Varieties Available

Zinfandel, Sangiovese, Malbec, Cabernet Franc, Albariño, Super Tuscan, Red Blends

Tasting Room

Saturdays and Sundays 11 AM to 5 PM

*Contact winery to confirm tasting room hours & currently available wines.

Correcaminos Vineyard Winery

RAMONA, CALIFORNIA

About the Winery

Correcaminos Vineyard specializes in crafting exquisite, hand-crafted wines sourced from estate and local grapes. Embracing the essence of the rural Ramona lifestyle, Correcaminos, meaning Roadrunner, is a testament to nature's beauty.

The talented winemakers behind this venture are Doug Robinson and Sue Robinson, eager to welcome visitors to share stories and savor the delightful Correcaminos wines. As proud members of the Harvest Hosts, they extend a unique invitation to those with Motorhomes/RVs for overnight stays at their Ramona vineyard and winery.

This exclusive opportunity offers wine tastings, a glimpse into their winemaking journey, and the chance to meet the hosts. Overnight visits are limited to one night, and prior arrangements, as well as proof of membership and registration upon arrival, are required. Correcaminos Vineyard invites you to join them for engaging, enjoyable, and educational events held right at the winery.

Location & Contact Info

1941 Lilac Road, Ramona, CA 92065

(760) 315-7444

correcaminosvineyard@gmail.com

https://correcaminosvineyard.com

Varieties Available

Cabernet Sauvignon, Malbec, Viognier, Zinfandel, Sangiovese, Symphony, Albariño

Tasting Room

Fridays, Saturdays and Sundays 12 PM to 5 PM

*Contact winery to confirm tasting room hours & currently available wines.

Winery
CRYSTAL HILL VINEYARD
RAMONA, CALIFORNIA

About the Winery

San Diego County's artisan winemaking at its finest is embodied by the Warner Family, known for their passion for artisan wines and agriculture. Their vineyards boast one-acre plots of Chardonnay, Cabernet Sauvignon, Merlot, Syrah, Sangiovese, Petite Sirah, Tempranillo, Cab Franc, and Barbera, demonstrating their commitment to producing premium single varietals in small, meticulously crafted batches.

The expansive landscape provides sweeping views of the valley, accommodating couples, families, and large groups for a relaxed and enjoyable full-service wine tasting experience. Visitors can also delve into wine cellars and vineyard tours. Crystal Hill serves as an ideal backdrop for gatherings, whether it's a birthday celebration, anniversary, corporate offsite, or an intimate get-together with friends.

Through small batches and slow fermentation at cold temperatures, they create complex wines with bold yet smooth flavors, including a unique line of single varietals aged in freshly emptied whiskey and bourbon barrels.

Location & Contact Info

24067 Old Julian Hwy, Ramona, CA 92065

(760) 440-5229

info@crystalhillvineyard.com

https://crystalhillvineyard.com

Varieties Available

Cabernet Sauvignon, Merlot, Pinot Gris, Rosé

Tasting Room

Fridays, Saturdays and Sundays 12 PM to 6 PM

*Contact winery to confirm tasting room hours & currently available wines.

Edwards Vineyard & Cellars

Winery

RAMONA, CALIFORNIA

About the Winery

Voted San Diego's Favorite Winery and celebrated as North County's prime producer of premium Syrah, Cabernet Sauvignon, and Petite Sirah estate-grown wines in the Ramona Valley AVA, Edwards Vineyard & Cellars is a cherished haven for wine enthusiasts. Rain or shine, visitors can follow the signs for year-round outdoor tastings amidst picturesque surroundings.

The Edwards Family embarked on their winemaking journey with the planting of their first Ramona Valley vineyard in 1990. Victor Edwards, the family patriarch, introduced his inaugural Petite Sirah in 1997, which remains their flagship wine. In March 2011, they proudly inaugurated their outdoor tasting patio, offering breathtaking vineyard and Ballena Valley views.

Despite the tragic loss of Victor in late 2021, his legacy lives on through the family's unwavering commitment to winemaking and their continued dedication to crafting future vintages in his memory.

Location & Contact Info

- 126502 CA-78, Ramona, CA 92065
- (760) 788-6800
- beth@edwardsvineyardandcellars.com
- https://www.edwardsvineyardandcellars.com

Varieties Available

Petite Sirah, Syrah, Cabernet Sauvignon

In near future: Grenache, Mourvèdre, Cinsaut, Counoise, Viognier

Tasting Room

Saturdays and Sundays 11 AM to 5 PM

Contact winery to confirm tasting room hours & currently available wines.

Hatfield Creek Winery

RAMONA, CALIFORNIA

About the Winery

Hatfield Creek Winery, nestled in Ramona Valley's scenic AVA, took root in 2006 and achieved bonded and licensed winery status by 2012. On a little over three acres, they proudly cultivate thriving Petite Sirah and Zinfandel grape varieties, consistently earning prestigious accolades.

Every Friday through Sunday, visitors are welcomed to partake in a delightful tasting experience at their inviting Tasting Room. Norm and Elaine, the passionate proprietors, acquired this 6-acre property within the Ramona AVA in 2006, channeling their zest for life, experience, and energy into the development of Hatfield Creek Winery. Their focus on red wines, particularly Estate-grown Zinfandel and Petite Sirah, has earned them international recognition, but their ultimate mission is to offer a captivating destination.

Enjoy the serene ambiance and rich history of the property, adorned with antiques indoors and remnants of an ancient native village, along with a unique 1961 Navy Jet crash site nestled in the vineyard.

Location & Contact Info

1625 Highway 78, Ramona, CA 92065

(760) 787-1102

elaine@hatfieldcreekvineyards.com

https://hatfieldcreekvineyards.com

Varieties Available

Estate Petite Sirah, Estate Zinfandel, Estate Malbec, blends and port

Tasting Room

Fridays, Saturdays and Sundays 11 AM to 5 PM

*Contact winery to confirm tasting room hours & currently available wines.

Mahogany Mountain Vineyard and Winery

RAMONA, CALIFORNIA

About the Winery

A charming family-owned and operated establishment, specializing in crafting limited production, handcrafted estate premium wines. Their portfolio features Barbera, Cabernet Sauvignon, Merlot, Mourvedre, Syrah, Zinfandel, Petit Verdot, Malbec and Muscat Canelli all cultivated in the picturesque Ramona Valley AVA of San Diego County, CA.

The Hargett family has called their 45-acre property home since 1989 and embarked on grape cultivation in 1996, eventually opening their winery's doors in 2004. Their son, a graduate of UC Irvine, brings his expertise in biology to both the vineyard and winemaking processes. Together, they meticulously tend to over 5 acres of vines, yielding 5 tons of fruit, and handle 100 percent of their inventory's bottling right on-site.

Mahogany Mountain has garnered acclaim with silver and gold medals in prominent competitions in New York, Sonoma, and Temecula. Locally, they've also earned prestigious awards at events like the annual Toast of the Coast Wine Festival and competitions organized by the Ramona Valley Vineyard Association.

Location & Contact Info

14905 Mussey Grade Rd, Ramona, CA 92065

(760) 788-7048

info@mahoganymountain.com

mahoganymountain.com

Varieties Available

Cabernet Sauvignon, Merlot, Syrah, Mourvedre, Malbec, Barbera, Dry Estate White (Muscat canelli), Port-style wine, Zinfandel, Red Blends and Sweet Muscat dessert wine

Tasting Room

Saturdays and Sundays 1 PM to 5 PM

Contact winery to confirm tasting room hours & currently available wines.

Winery

MERMAID VALLEY VINEYARD

RAMONA, CALIFORNIA

About the Winery

Nestled amid the picturesque mountains just beyond San Diego, Mermaid Valley Vineyard benefits from abundant sunshine and refreshing coastal breezes, creating an idyllic setting for crafting exceptional wines. Established in 2013 by Kim and Scott Flinn, the vineyard saw the planting of over 3,000 vines in 2014, with its inaugural commercial harvest gracing the scene in 2016.

Mermaid Valley Vineyard takes pride in being 100% estate-grown and produced, boasting an annual production of 700 cases. Scott Flinn has earned recognition for his winemaking prowess with multiple award-winning wines. The 2018 Siren's Song, a captivating Rhone-style blend of Grenache, Syrah, and Mourvèdre, secured double gold, Best Blended Red Rhone, and the prestigious Best of San Diego County title at the 2022 Toast of the Coast Wine Competition. The vineyard's 2017 Late Harvest Zinfandel, a delectable dessert wine, also claimed double gold in the 2020 competition. As well as their 2023 Seadog red table wine winning double gold at the International Sommelier Conference.

Location & Contact Info

18420 Highland Valley Rd, Ramona, CA 92065

(760) 315-9011

mermaidvineyard@gmail.com

mermaidvalleyvineyard.com

Varieties Available

Mourvèdre Rosé, Zinfandel, Sauvignon Blanc, Viognier, Grenache Rosé, Merlot, Syrah, Grenache, Negrette, Petit Syrah

Tasting Room

Saturdays 11 AM to 5 PM

Proudly Veteran Owned

Contact winery to confirm tasting room hours & currently available wines.

Milagro Farm Vineyards and Winery

RAMONA, CALIFORNIA

About the Winery

Nestled in Ramona Valley, their property graces an undulating landscape adorned with magnificent granite boulders and the graceful presence of Coast Live Oak trees. Abundant onsite wells and nutrient-rich granite soil nurture their vines.

With over 10,000 vines yielding 11 varietals, Milagro's wines embody the unique character of Ramona Valley. Led by European-style viticulturist Thomas Egli, and joined by local talents Tony and Olga Ramos, their winemaking team is dedicated to expressing the essence of their land in every bottle. Milagro's unwavering passion for excellence fuels their commitment to sharing extraordinary offerings.

As you explore their property, you'll be treated to panoramic views, rolling hills, and mineral-rich soils, all contributing to the creation of award-winning wines and memorable experiences. From Chardonnay to Super Tuscan, Sauvignon Blanc to Rosé, their exceptional winemaking blends tradition and innovation to offer a diverse tapestry of flavors and aromas that define the unique charm of Milagro.

Location & Contact Info

18750 Littlepage Rd, Ramona, CA 92065

(760) 800-3184

tastingroom@milagrowinery.com

https://www.milagrowinery.com

Varieties Available

Cabernet Sauvignon, Merlot, Sangiovese, Chardonnay, Pinot Gris, Sauvignon Blanc, Rosé of Sangiovese, Sparkling Brut Rosé, Barbera, Super Tuscan blend, Bordeaux blend

Tasting Room

Saturdays and Sundays 12 PM to 6 PM

*Contact winery to confirm tasting room hours & currently available wines.

Old Julian Vineyards & Winery

RAMONA, CALIFORNIA

About the Winery

Old Julian Vineyards & Winery stands as a renowned establishment, celebrated for its iconic Red Barn and its distinction in crafting fine wines and brandy. The talented brother-and-sister team of Lee and Shelli Montgomery behind this winery continually presents a diverse array of high-quality, yet affordable, wines and brandy.

Nestled within the picturesque landscape of Ramona, you'll find varietals both familiar to the region and unique, alongside special blends meticulously crafted by the winery. Their impressive vineyard encompasses 7,000 vines, representing a rich diversity of grapes such as Syrah, Cabernet Sauvignon, Merlot, Malbec, Petite Syrah, Sauvignon Blanc, Viognier, and Muscat.

With open arms for furry friends, guests are welcome to bring their leashed and well-behaved pets, creating an inviting atmosphere where you can indulge in picnics paired with their award-winning wines while relishing breathtaking views of the sprawling vineyards, rolling hills, and the valley beyond.

Location & Contact Info

25352 Old Julian Hwy, Ramona, CA 92065

(949) 374-7700

oldjulianvineyards@gmail.com

https://www.oldjulianvineyards.com

Varieties Available

Cabernet Sauvignon, Merlot, Syrah, Viognier, Sauvignon Blanc, Rosé, Cabernet Franc, Petit Verdot, Petite Syrah, red blends

Also a selection of handcrafted Brandies!

Tasting Room

Fridays, Saturdays and Sundays 12 PM to 6 PM

Contact winery to confirm tasting room hours & currently available wines.

Pamo Valley Winery

RAMONA, CALIFORNIA

About the Winery

Pamo Valley Winery's story begins with the establishment of their Syrah vineyard overlooking the picturesque Pamo Valley in 2000, which inspired their distinctive name. In 2007, they embarked on a new journey, relocating to a scenic mountainside location on Black Canyon Road in Ramona, California.

Jennifer J. Lane, Proprietor & Winemaker, is fueled by a profound passion for crafting premium wines that captivate the senses. Guided by the belief that wine, inherently feminine, is a gift from Mother Nature, Jennifer's winemaking philosophy emphasizes creating approachable and delightful wines for a broad spectrum of wine enthusiasts. Her wines are characterized by their fruit-forward profiles and soft, harmonious finishes, avoiding overpowering tannins.

Pamo Valley's meticulous, handcrafted winemaking process preserves timeless traditions, and their tasting room welcomes visitors to enjoy a glass of wine in the company of their furry friends.

Location & Contact Info

636 Main Street, Ramona, CA 92065

(760) 271-3090

info@pamovalleywinery.com

https://pamovalleywinery.com

Varieties Available

Grenache Rosé, Sauvignon Blanc, Chardonnay, Estate Primitivo, Cabernet Sauvignon, Cab Franc, Petit Verdot, Petite Sirah, Syrah, Dessert Style Port

Tasting Room

Sunday, Monday, Tuesday, Wednesday ~ 2 PM - 6 PM
Thursday ~ 2 PM - 9 PM; Friday & Saturday ~ 2 PM - 8 PM

*Contact winery to confirm tasting room hours & currently available wines.

Winery
POPPAEA VINEYARD
RAMONA, CALIFORNIA

About the Winery

Poppaea Vineyard and Winery, a charming family-operated boutique winery was founded in 2009 by John Saunders, along with his wife Marion and son Ben. Their vision was to rejuvenate a wildfire-affected property on the outskirts of Ramona Valley by cultivating Italian red wine grape varietals inspired by their travels through Italy.

Drawing from John's background in pharmaceutical chemistry, the winemaking at Poppaea combines scientific rigor with old-world Italian traditions. The vineyard originally featured six Italian red varietals, including Sangiovese, Montepulciano, Nebbiolo, Barbera, Primitivo, and Sagrantino.

Visitors are welcomed to enjoy a tasting paddle of their Italian varietal wines, complemented by stunning views of Ramona Valley and Mt. Woodson peak. There are indoor and outdoor seating options, including "*The Island*," a private shaded tasting area, and a picnic table in their experimental vineyard block.

Location & Contact Info

25643 Old Julian Hwy, Ramona, CA 92065

(858) 357-1741

poppaeasabina13@gmail.com

https://poppaeavineyard.com

Varieties Available

Poppaea Rosso, Montepulciano, Barbera, Primitivo, Proserpina, Sagrantino, Poppaea Rosé

Tasting Room

Fridays 2-5 PM, Saturdays & Sundays 12-6 PM

*Contact winery to confirm tasting room hours & currently available wines.

Principe di Tricase Winery

RAMONA, CALIFORNIA

About the Winery

The Principe di Tricase Winery estate offers an array of inviting spaces, each with its unique atmosphere to cater to various preferences. From the expansive patio to secluded corners and three enchanting natural grottos adorned with pomegranate trees, there's a perfect spot for every guest to unwind and savor the tranquil countryside ambiance.

Their winemaking philosophy revolves around the production of natural wines, exclusively crafted from local grapes. With 13 different estate varietals, including predominantly Italian ones, and an additional 8 sourced from trusted local growers, they have cultivated strong relationships over the years.

As a diverse and welcoming family-owned establishment, Principe di Tricase Winery encompasses more than just vines; it's a working farm and a delightful Christmas Tree Farm. Here, they open their hearts to visitors and their beloved dogs and horses, recognizing these faithful companions as cherished members of the family.

Location & Contact Info

18425 Highland Valley Rd, Ramona, CA 92065

(858) 336-0663

wine@pineandwine.com

https://www.pineandwine.com

Tasting Room

Saturdays and Sundays 12 PM to 5 PM

Varieties Available

Malvasia, Fiano, Aglianico, Nebbiolo, Sangiovese, Aleatico, Piedirosso, Nero d'Avola, Primitivo, Teroldego, Dolcetto, Sagrantino, Cabernet Sauvignon, Petite Sirah, Zinfandel, Cabernet Franc, Sauvignon Blanc, Chardonnay, Merlot, Syrah, Malbec

*Contact winery to confirm tasting room hours & currently available wines.

Ramona Ranch Vineyard & Winery

RAMONA, CALIFORNIA

About the Winery

Nestled in the heart of the Ramona Valley AVA, this family-owned winery is committed to crafting wines that stand the test of time. They prioritize sustainability, with wind turbines, solar panels, owl boxes, and an insectary that has earned them the Certified Wildlife Habitat recognition from the National Wildlife Federation; as well as a Certificate of Sustainability from the California Wine Institute.

Ramona Ranch sources grapes from their estate vineyards and select local growers known for their dedication to the land. Their award-winning wines, including the Double-Gold, Best of Class Estate Tannat, showcases the care and devotion to the terroir.

Led by husband and wife team, Micole Moore and Teri Kerns, this family venture invites you to experience the beauty of the Ramona Valley and the warm wine community with the invitation, *"Vaya con Vino"* ~ come and embrace the enchantment of this winery, where sustainability meets extraordinary wines.

Location & Contact Info

23578 Highway 78,
Ramona, CA 92065

(760) 789-1622

teri@ramonaranchwines.com

https://ramonaranchwines.com

Varieties Available

Sauvignon Blanc, Albariño, Viognier, Rosé of Sangiovese, Aglianico, Super Tuscan, Montepulciano, Tannat, Bourbon Barrel Syrah, Sangiovese, & more

Tasting Room

Fridays, Saturdays and Sundays 11 AM to 6 PM
Thursdays & Mondays 1 PM to 5 PM

*Contact winery to confirm tasting room hours & currently available wines.

Rancho San Martín Winery

RAMONA, CALIFORNIA

About the Winery

In 2010, native San Diegans Ginny and Gary Boney established Rancho San Martín Winery, nestled in Highland Valley on the west end of Ramona, inspired by their love for the local outdoors and landscapes. They embarked on a journey to cultivate their vineyard, learning from experienced vintners in the Ramona Valley and emphasizing the importance of quality grapes in crafting exceptional wine.

Visitors can unwind in the serene countryside atmosphere and savor Italian and Spanish varietals carefully chosen to harmonize with the local terroir. With wines aged in barrels for over two years, Rancho San Martín Winery promises a delightful tasting experience, striving to offer the best in the valley.

Their vineyard boasts a diverse selection of varietals, including Sangiovese, Brunello clone of Sangiovese, Tempranillo, Syrah, Grenache, Cabernet Sauvignon, Rosé, and blends. Winemakers Ginny and Gary Boney's dedication shines through in each bottle.

Location & Contact Info

17249 Sundance Dr, Ramona, CA 92065

(760) 650-6851

ginny.rsmwinery@gmail.com

https://rsmwines.com

Varieties Available

Albariño, Rosé of Sangiovese, Rosé of Tempranillo, Estate Tempranillo, Maggiore, Liggero Ma Ricco, Cabernet Sauvignon, Grenache, Syrah, GSM, Mourvèdre, Cabernet Franc, Sangiovese, and some red blends

Tasting Room

Saturdays and Sundays 12 PM to 5 PM
Gate code #1957

Contact winery to confirm tasting room hours & currently available wines.

Rashelica Winery & Art Garden

RAMONA, CALIFORNIA

About the Winery

Nestled in the picturesque hills of Ramona Valley, Rashelica Winery & Art offers a unique cultural experience that seamlessly combines award-winning handcrafted wines, a remarkable collection of world-class sculptures, and live performances by local musicians.

As you step into Rashelica, a captivating array of sculptures graces the entrance to the tasting terrace, welcoming you to this serene outdoor setting that provides panoramic views of vineyard-covered hills, encouraging guests to unwind and savor the moment.

Rashelica Winery & Art is not merely a winery but a destination that invites visitors to appreciate the seamless harmony between fine art, exceptional wine, and the enchanting beauty of Ramona Valley. Jaime Chaljon, Salerno Winery's proprietor, has thoughtfully curated this artistic haven, adorning the sculpture garden with over 30 treasured pieces from renowned artists, elevating the overall cultural experience.

Location & Contact Info

17948 CA-67,
Ramona, CA 92065

(619) 548-0941

https://www.rashelicagarden.com

Varieties Available

Ruby Cabernet, Petit Sirah, Malbec, Port

Tasting Room

Saturdays and Sundays 11 AM to 6 PM

*Contact winery to confirm tasting room hours & currently available wines.

Winery
SCENIC VALLEY RANCH VINEYARDS
RAMONA, CALIFORNIA

About the Winery

Scenic Valley Ranch, a charming boutique winery situated on the outskirts of Ramona in the scenic Ballena Valley, offers visitors a delightful wine-tasting experience. Their wines are meticulously crafted from hand-harvested grapes sourced from both their estate vineyards and select Ramona Valley vineyards.

Dennis and Sherry McGrath introduced wine tastings at Scenic Valley Ranch Vineyard in May 2022, offering wine enthusiasts the chance to savor their exquisite creations. Notably, their wines have recently earned Silver medals at the prestigious 2022 San Francisco Chronicle Wine Competition, with their 2020 Cabernet Franc, 2020 Petite Sirah and 2019 *"An Old Flame"* Flame Tokay.

Whether you're seeking to entertain friends, enjoy a relaxing picnic, or share a romantic afternoon, Scenic Valley Ranch's tasting patio is the perfect setting. Here, guests can explore the diverse range of wines and gain insight into the winemaking process directly from the owners themselves.

Location & Contact Info

27012 Scenic Valley Rd, Ramona, CA 92065

(619) 884-3514

scenicvalleyranch@gmail.com

https://www.scenicvalleyranch.com

Varieties Available

Cabernet Franc, Merlot, Rosé of Merlot, Malbec, Petite Sirah, Albariño, Ballena Blanco, Flame Tokay

Tasting Room

Saturdays and Sundays 11 AM to 6 PM

Contact winery to confirm tasting room hours & currently available wines.

Schwaesdall Winery

RAMONA, CALIFORNIA

About the Winery

Schwaesdall Winery, founded by San Diego native John Schwaesdall, has a rich winemaking history rooted in Ramona's old vineyards, some of which date back to the 1950s.

The vineyard's unique location among magnificent granite boulders, prevalent in the Ramona/Mt. Woodson region, offers visitors an opportunity to admire natural sculptures amidst the 6-acre property, with picturesque views of Iron Mountain in the distance. As you step into the tasting room, you'll notice that it's housed in the first permitted commercial straw bale building in San Diego County, with walls constructed from straw bales.

Established in 1996, Schwaesdall Winery holds the distinction of being the first bonded winery in Ramona. Their wine portfolio includes a variety of whites, reds, and ports. Whether you're seeking a leisurely wine tasting, a scenic escape, or a chance to mingle with the passionate winemakers, Schwaesdall Winery offers a warm and welcoming setting for wine enthusiasts.

Location & Contact Info

17677 Rancho De Oro Dr, Ramona, CA 92065

(760) 789-7542

shirley@schwaesdallwinery.com

https://www.schwaesdallwinery.com

Varieties Available

Merlot, Chardonnay, Cabernet Sauvignon, "Portly Pig" Port, Orange Muscat Port, "Dump Truck" Zin Port, "Miss Piggy" Port, as well as red and white blends

Tasting Room

Saturdays and Sundays 11 AM to 6 PM

*Contact winery to confirm tasting room hours & currently available wines.

Winery
SKY VALLEY CELLARS
RAMONA, CALIFORNIA

About the Winery

Sky Valley Cellars, a family-owned and operated vineyard and boutique winery, is nestled in Ramona's rolling hills, just a short drive from the San Diego Coastal area. Perched at 1600 feet elevation, this winery benefits from coastal Pacific breezes, a sunny Southern California climate, and unique rocky slopes, all contributing to crafting premium wines.

Notably, their Italian Style Rosé earned exceptional recognition with 96 points, Best of Class, and a Double Gold award at the 2022 OC Fair Commercial Wine competition among 2400 California wines.

In their continual pursuit of excellence, Sky Valley Cellars made the strategic decision to enlist the expertise of head winemaker Andrew Wisniewski, who is dedicated to building Sky Valley Cellars' reputation as a producer of high-quality wine within the Ramona AVA, ensuring that each bottle reflects the winery's commitment to excellence.

Location & Contact Info

- 16729 Sky Valley Dr, Ramona, CA 92065
- (760) 896-2685
- info@skyvalleycellars.com
- https://www.skyvalleycellars.com

Varieties Available

Syrah, Petite Sirah, Sangiovese, Rosé, Dessert wine

Tasting Room

Fridays 3 PM - 6 PM; Saturday & Sunday 1 PM - 6 PM

*Contact winery to confirm tasting room hours & currently available wines.

Winery

SUNRISE VINEYARDS

RAMONA, CALIFORNIA

About the Winery

Sunrise Vineyards exemplifies a dedication to crafting exceptional wines, producing all their offerings from grapes grown either on-site or within a 1.5-mile radius of the winery, capturing the essence of the Ramona Valley AVA's western region.

Located strategically on a ridge between Poway and the Ramona Valley, this winery enjoys refreshing ocean breezes, creating an ideal microclimate for grape cultivation. Meticulously planted grape varietals, including Sangiovese, Cabernet Sauvignon, Touriga Nacional, and Sauvignon Blanc, thrive in the nutrient-rich granite soil.

Their commitment to quality extends from the vineyard to the winemaking process, with red wines spending 1-3 years in barrels, depending on factors like barrel wood, varietal, and winemaker preferences. Furthermore, their white wines are crafted to preserve their fresh, light, fruity flavors and crispness, with no malolactic fermentation or oak aging, ensuring a delightful and refreshing wine experience.

Location & Contact Info

16620 Highland Valley Rd, Ramona, CA 92065

(858) 334-9955

sunrisevineyards@gmail.com

https://www.sunrisevineyardsandwinery.com

Varieties Available

Sangiovese, Merlot, Cabernet Sauvignon, Sauvignon Blanc, Viognier, Syrah, Grenache Blanc

Tasting Room

Saturday and Sunday ~ 12 PM to 7 PM

*Contact winery to confirm tasting room hours & currently available wines.

Three Hills Winery

RAMONA, CALIFORNIA

About the Winery

At Three Hills Winery, guests are in for a unique and delightful wine-tasting experience in the heart of Ramona. With tasting menus featuring 5 to 7 carefully curated wines, visitors can embark on a flavorful journey that covers the spectrum of wine styles.

From light, fruity, and crisp white wines to exquisite rosés and an extensive selection of red wines, including the prestigious gold medal-winning Super Tuscan, Merlot, Zinfandel, Cabernet, Syrah, Double Trouble Port, and Spoiled Rotten Dessert Wine, there's something to please every palate.

As guests explore the charming 9-acre estate, they'll discover neatly groomed acres with walking trails, secluded seating areas, a serene lake, a picturesque bridge, and even a seasonal 50-foot waterfall. With the flexibility to bring your own picnic and well-mannered leashed dogs and kids welcome, Three Hills Winery offers a welcoming and relaxed atmosphere, perfect for enjoying wine and quality time with friends.

Location & Contact Info

16805 Highland Valley Rd, Ramona, CA 92065

(619) 507-7920

Info@ThreeHillsWinery.com

https://www.threehillswinery.com

Varieties Available

Picpoul Blanc, Pinot Grigio, Sangiovese Rosé, Ruby Rosé, Merlot, Cabernet Sauvignon, Zinfandel, Syrah, Red Blends, Port Style red, Port Style white, Limoncello, Sangria

Tasting Room

Saturday and Sunday ~ 11:30 AM to 5:30 PM

*Contact winery to confirm tasting room hours & currently available wines.

Winery
Turtle Rock Ridge
RAMONA, CALIFORNIA

About the Winery

Nestled in the breathtaking backcountry of San Diego County, Turtle Rock Ridge is a picturesque Ramona winery that derives its name from the majestic granite monolith that presides over a vineyard and tasting terrace.

With a strong commitment to producing exceptional wines, Turtle Rock Ridge sources the finest grapes from both its own vineyard and local growers within the Ramona and broader California wine region. The winery boasts an impressive selection of red and white wines, many of which have earned prestigious awards, a testament to their dedication to quality.

Turtle Rock Ridge also stands firmly behind the principles of Reduce, Reuse, and Recycle, implementing organic farming techniques that minimize resource usage while crafting premium wines. The winemaking expertise of Laurie Wagner and Ian Vaux is at the heart of Turtle Rock Ridge's success, and visitors are welcomed to explore the vineyard, and tour the wine cave where these vines have been nurtured from bud break to harvest.

Location & Contact Info

18351 Woods Hill Lane, Ramona, CA 92065

(760) 789-5555

tasting@turtlerockridge.com

https://www.turtlerockridge.com

Varieties Available

Estate Zinfandel, Sangiovese, Chardonnay, Cabernet Sauvignon, Syrah, Cabernet Franc, Red blends, and Premium Sangria

Tasting Room

Thursday and Friday 2-6 PM
Saturday and Sunday 12- 6 PM

*Contact winery to confirm tasting room hours & currently available wines.

Vina Ramona Winery

RAMONA, CALIFORNIA

About the Winery

Vina Ramona Winery, set on an 11-acre vineyard, offers a charming atmosphere with scenic seating areas, shade, and a diverse wine tasting menu featuring six exceptional wines.

Situated on a secluded wooded property in Ramona, just off Old Julian Highway, this winery provides a unique experience. The tasting room, a converted trailer with a speakeasy charm, opens to inviting outdoor seating areas among oak trees and boulders, offering picturesque views.

Owner and winemaker Ben Payne, known for his winemaking prowess developed over a decade, warmly welcomes guests and shares insights into his new wines, which recently garnered recognition with three medals in the RVVA Wine Tasting Competition, including gold for the Cabernet Sauvignon and bronze for the Merlot and Petite Syrah.

Location & Contact Info

657 East Old Julian Hwy, Ramona, CA 92065

(760) 315-8068

info@vinaramona.com

https://vinaramona.com

Varieties Available

Rosé, Chardonnay, Merlot, Cabernet Sauvignon, Petite Sirah, "Neglect" Petite Sirah/Malbec blend, "Late Z" dessert

Tasting Room

Saturday and Sunday 1 - 5 PM

*Contact winery to confirm tasting room hours & currently available wines.

Winery
Vineyard Grant James
RAMONA, CALIFORNIA

About the Winery

Vineyard Grant James's expansive valley views provide an ideal backdrop for nurturing various grape varietals, such as Syrah, Merlot, Sangiovese, Orange Muscat, Greco, Refosco, and Nebbiolo. Located in Ramona, California, this inviting vineyard beckons wine enthusiasts to relish its wines and share in the joys of fine wine and authentic camaraderie.

Devoted to the art of pure winemaking, Vineyard Grant James meticulously crafts each bottle to capture the essence of their labor and the unique terroir that defines it. They source grapes from both their estate and local vineyards in Ramona Valley, preserving the authentic boutique quality of Ramona's wine scene.

They offer a diverse collection of popular and award-winning selections, including Viognier, Rosé of Syrah, Sangiovese, Zinfandel, Nebbiolo, Merlot, Syrah, and Petite Sirah, each bottle a testament to Vineyard Grant James' unwavering commitment to crafting memorable wine experiences.

Location & Contact Info

25260 Old Julian Hwy, Ramona, CA 92065

(760) 206-3481

info@vineyardgrantjames.com

https://www.vineyardgrantjames.com

Varieties Available

Cabernet Sauvignon, Merlot, Zinfandel, Sangiovese, Chardonnay, Syrah, Viognier, Rosé, Phoenix (blend), Lacerta (blend), Aquarius (blend), Cabernet Franc, Alicante Bouschet

Tasting Room

Friday through Sunday 12 - 6PM

*Contact winery to confirm tasting room hours & currently available wines.

Woof'n Rosé Winery

RAMONA, CALIFORNIA

About the Winery

Nestled on a north-facing hillside with captivating views of the Ramona Valley AVA, Woof'n Rose Winery is a labor of love owned and operated by Stephen and Marilyn Kahle, who receive assistance from their three sons, their respective families and all of their dogs.

The winery's name, inspired by the Kahle's love for dogs and the surrounding Rose bushes, reflects their deep connection to both. Woof'n Rose Winery is dedicated to crafting red wines exclusively from Ramona Valley grapes, with the majority being estate-grown on-site.

The winery produces an annual output of 300 to 350 cases, showcasing its expertise in Cabernet Franc. In addition to Cabernet Franc, the small vineyards cultivate classic Bordeaux varietals such as Cabernet Sauvignon, Merlot, Malbec, Petit Verdot, and Carmenere, along with other varietals like Grenache Noir, Alicante Bouschet, and Montepulciano. Each wine is a reflection of these distinct varietals and their skillful blends.

Location & Contact Info

17073 Garjan Lane, Ramona, CA 92065

(760) 788-4818

marilyn@woofnrose.com

https://woofnrose.com

Varieties Available

Cabernet Franc, Merlot, Cabernet Sauvignon, Petit Verdot, Malbec, Alicante Bouschet, Montepulciano, Grenache Noir, Carmenere, Estate Puppy Love (blend), Estate Happy Tails (blend), Estate Eglantine (blend), Estate Late Harvest Puppy Love (dessert), Neuf Anges (dessert)

Tasting Room

Saturday & Sunday - 11 AM to 5:30 PM

*Contact winery to confirm tasting room hours & currently available wines.

Recipe Index

Albóndigas (main, Tempranillo), 204
Amaretto Bliss (cocktail, Zinfandel), 88
Aperol Spritz (cocktail, Syrah), 140
Apple Cranberry Galette (dessert, Viognier), 184
Asparagus Salad (side, Sauvignon Blanc), 252
Baby Artichokes w/ Tomato Coulis (side, Syrah), 146
Bacon Jalapeño Poppers (appetizer, Zinfandel), 90
Baked Macaroni & Cheese (side, Cabernet Sauvignon), 18
Baked Penne w/ Prosciutto & Fontina (main, Cabernet Franc), 256
BBQ Pulled Pork (main, Petit Verdot), 258
Beef Fajitas (main, Zinfandel), 100
Beef Stroganoff (main, Cabernet Sauvignon), 26
Beef Tenderloin in Mushroom Sauce (main, Zinfandel), 98
Berry Vino Smash (cocktail, Cabernet Sauvignon), 8
Blue Cheese Logs (appetizer, Syrah), 144
Bourbon Ham Balls (appetizer, Sangiovese), 118
Brandied Mushroom Paté (appetizer, Zinfandel), 92
Brandy Blend (cocktail, Malbec), 216
Brandy Bliss (cocktail, Sangiovese), 112
Bread Pudding (dessert, Merlot), 80
Buffalo Chicken Biscuits (appetizer, Merlot), 66
Buffalo Chicken Dip (appetizer, Chardonnay), 40
Cabana Cooler (cocktail, Chardonnay), 36
Cannoli (dessert, Sangiovese), 134
Caprese Salad (side, Zinfandel), 94
Carne Asada w/ Grilled Onions (main, Malbec), 230
Cheesy Au Gratin Potatoes & Ham (main, Petite Sirah), 254
Cherry Flaugnarde (dessert, Syrah), 158
Cherry Whiskey Sour (cocktail, Sangiovese), 114
Chicken & Bacon Roll-Ups (appetizer, Syrah), 142
Chicken & Dumplings (main, Chardonnay), 46
Chicken & Mushroom Fricassee (main, Syrah), 152
Chicken Cordon Bleu Casserole (main, Viognier), 180
Chicken Française (main, Viognier), 178
Chicken-Fried Steak (main, Merlot), 78
Chili Mac (main, Merlot), 74
Chocolate Pound Cake (dessert, Cabernet Sauvignon), 30
Chocolate-Bourbon Pecan Pie (dessert, Tempranillo), 210
Cognac Fusion (cocktail, Malbec), 218
Coq au Vin (main, Syrah), 150
Creamy Spinach Artichoke Dip (appetizer, Chardonnay), 38
Crepes (dessert, Viognier), 186
Crush Punch (cocktail, Cabernet Sauvignon), 10
Cucumber-Stuffed Cherry Tomatoes (appetizer, Sangiovese), 116
Dark Chocolate Molten Cupcakes (dessert, Port), 262
Dark Chocolate Truffles (dessert, Malbec), 236
Double Dark Chocolate Cookies (dessert, Malbec), 238
Double-Chocolate Mousse Cake (dessert, Zinfandel), 106
Eggplant Parmesan (main, Sangiovese), 128
Espinacas con Garbanzos (side, Tempranillo), 198
Fondant Potatoes (side, Viognier), 172
Fudge Brownies (dessert, Tempranillo), 212
Garlic & Jalapeno Bison Burger (main, Malbec), 234
Gin Symphony (cocktail, Syrah), 138
Glazed Carrot Medley (side, Chardonnay), 42

Green Bean Casserole (side, Merlot), 68
Green Beans Almondine (side, Syrah), 148
Grilled Lobster (main, Chardonnay), 52
Grilled Mushroom Antipasto Salad (side, Grenache), 250
Grilled Peaches (dessert, Zinfandel), 108
Grilled Portobello Mushroom Steaks (main, Malbec), 228
Grilled Ribeye Steak (main, Malbec), 232
Herbed-Crusted Cod w/ Pea Puree (main, Chardonnay), 50
Kalimotxo (cocktail, Merlot), 60
Lemonade Fizz (cocktail, Zinfandel), 86
Loaded Mashed Potatoes (side, Malbec), 224
Lobster Thermidor w/ Béchamel Sauce (main, Viognier), 182
Meatloaf (main, Cabernet Sauvignon), 24
Merlot Mary (cocktail, Merlot), 62
Mexican Zucchini Boats (side, Sangiovese), 122
Olive Tapenade (appetizer, Viognier), 170
Orange Soufflé (dessert, Chardonnay), 56
Pan-Seared Salmon (main, Viognier), 176
Peach Cobbler (dessert, Chardonnay), 54
Peach Sangria (cocktail, Albariño), 242
Pineapple Upside-Down Cake (dessert, Merlot), 82
Poke Nachos (appetizer, Albariño), 246
Pork Marsala w/ Mushrooms (main, Zinfandel), 102
Pork Ragù Over Creamy Polenta (main, Sangiovese), 126
Pork Tenderloin w/ Chutney (main, Cabernet Franc), 260
Puchero (main, Tempranillo), 206
Raspberry Sorbet (dessert, Rosé), 264
Ratatouille (main, Syrah), 156
Roasted Baby Potatoes (side, Cabernet Sauvignon), 16
Roasted Brussels Sprouts (side, Zinfandel), 96
Roasted Marrow Bones (appetizer, Malbec), 222
Salted H.P Chocolate Tarte Tatin (dessert, Syrah), 160
Sausage Rolls (appetizer, Merlot), 64
Scallops w/ Citrus Drizzle (appetizer, Viognier), 168
Seafood Paella (main, Tempranillo), 202
Sesame Beef Skewers (main, Sangiovese), 124
Short Rib Bourguignon (main, Syrah), 154
Shrimp & Grits (main, Chardonnay), 48
Shrimp Cocktail (cocktail, Malbec), 220
Singapore Sling (cocktail, Tempranillo), 192
Sloppy Joes (main, Merlot), 72
Slow Cooker Turkey Chili (main, Merlot), 76
Smk. Salmon & Cucumber (appetizer, Sauvignon Blanc), 248
Spinach au Gratin (side, Viognier), 174
Spinach Lasagna w/ Ricotta (main, Sangiovese), 130
Steak Frites (main, Cabernet Sauvignon), 22
Steak Tartare (appetizer, Tempranillo), 196
Strawberry Shortcake (dessert, Cabernet Sauvignon), 28
Sunshine Sipper (cocktail, Chardonnay), 34
Swedish Meatballs (main, Cabernet Sauvignon), 20
Sweet 'n' Tangy Chicken Wings (appetizer, Tempranillo), 194
Tiramisù (dessert, Sangiovese), 132
Tomato-Herb Grilled Tilapia (main, Tempranillo), 208
Turkey & Mushroom Risotto (side, Sangiovese), 120
Turkey Enchiladas (main, Zinfandel), 104
Vegetable Tortilla (side, Tempranillo), 200
Vino Guacamole (appetizer, Cabernet Sauvignon), 14

Recipe & Winery Varietals Index

recipe index cont...

Visions (cocktail, Viognier), 166
Vodka Elixir (cocktail, Viognier), 164
Waldorf Salad (side, Chardonnay), 44
Whiskey Fusion (cocktail, Tempranillo), 190
White Sangria (cocktail, Sauvignon Blanc), 244
Wild Rice & Mush. Stuffed Peppers (side, Malbec), 226
Wine Crostini (appetizer, Cabernet Sauvignon), 12
Zucchini Parmesan (side, Merlot), 70

Wineries that carry Wines Listed in Cookbook:

ALBARIÑO
Chuparosa Vineyards
Correcaminos Vineyard
Ramona Ranch Vineyard & Winery
Rancho San Martín Winery
Scenic Valley Ranch Vineyards

CABERNET FRANC
Castelli & Pizarro Family Winery
Chuparosa Vineyards
Old Julian Vineyards & Winery
Pamo Valley Winery
Principe di Tricase Winery
Rancho San Martín Winery
Scenic Valley Ranch Vineyards
Turtle Rock Ridge
Vineyard Grant James
Woof'n Rose Winery

CABERNET SAUVIGNON
Barrel 1 Winery
Cactus Star Vineyard at Scaredy Cat Ranch
Castelli & Pizarro Family Winery
Correcaminos Vineyard
Crystal Hill Vineyard
Edwards Vineyard & Cellars
Mahogany Mountain Vineyard and Winery
Milagro Farm Vineyards and Winery
Old Julian Vineyards & Winery
Pamo Valley Winery
Principe di Tricase Winery
Rancho San Martín Winery
Schwaesdall Winery
Sunrise Vineyards
Three Hills Winery
Turtle Rock Ridge
Vina Ramona
Vineyard Grant James
Woof'n Rose Winery

CHARDONNAY
Castelli & Pizarro Family Winery
Milagro Farm Vineyards and Winery
Pamo Valley Winery
Principe di Tricase Winery
Schwaesdall Winery
Turtle Rock Ridge
Vina Ramona
Vineyard Grant James

GRENACHE
Edwards Vineyard & Cellars
Mermaid Valley Vineyard
Rancho San Martín Winery

MALBEC
Cactus Star Vineyard at Scaredy Cat Ranch
Chuparosa Vineyards
Correcaminos Vineyard
Hatfield Creek Winery
Mahogany Mountain Vineyard and Winery
Principe di Tricase Winery
Rashelica Winery & Art Garden
Scenic Valley Ranch Vineyards
Woof'n Rose Winery

MERLOT
Barrel 1 Winery
Crystal Hill Vineyard
Mahogany Mountain Vineyard and Winery
Mermaid Valley Vineyard
Milagro Farm Vineyards and Winery
Old Julian Vineyards & Winery
Principe di Tricase Winery
Scenic Valley Ranch Vineyards
Schwaesdall Winery
Sunrise Vineyards
Three Hills Winery
Vina Ramona
Vineyard Grant James
Woof'n Rose Winery

PETIT VERDOT
Cactus Star Vineyard at Scaredy Cat Ranch
Castelli & Pizarro Family Winery
Old Julian Vineyards & Winery
Pamo Valley Winery
Woof'n Rose Winery

Winery Varietals Index (cont.)

PETITE SIRAH
Castelli & Pizarro Family Winery
Edwards Vineyard & Cellars
Hatfield Creek Winery
Mermaid Valley Vineyard
Old Julian Vineyards & Winery
Pamo Valley Winery
Principe di Tricase Winery
Rashelica Winery & Art Garden
Scenic Valley Ranch Vineyards
Sky Valley Cellars
Vina Ramona

PORT OR PORT STYLE
Rashelica Winery & Art Garden
Schwaesdall Winery
Three Hills Winery

ROSÉ
Barrel 1 Winery
Crystal Hill Vineyard
Mermaid Valley Vineyard
Milagro Farm Vineyards and Winery
Old Julian Vineyards & Winery
Poppaea Vineyard
Ramona Ranch Vineyard & Winery
Rancho San Martín Winery
Scenic Valley Ranch Vineyards
Sky Valley Cellars
Three Hills Winery
Vina Ramona
Vineyard Grant James

SANGIOVESE
Castelli & Pizarro Family Winery
Chuparosa Vineyards
Correcaminos Vineyard
Milagro Farm Vineyards and Winery
Principe di Tricase Winery
Ramona Ranch Vineyard & Winery
Rancho San Martín Winery
Sky Valley Cellars
Sunrise Vineyards
Turtle Rock Ridge
Vineyard Grant James

SAUVIGNON BLANC
Mermaid Valley Vineyard
Milagro Farm Vineyards and Winery
Old Julian Vineyards & Winery
Pamo Valley Winery
Principe di Tricase Winery
Ramona Ranch Vineyard & Winery
Sunrise Vineyards
Scallops with Citrus Drizzle
Scenic Valley Ranch Vineyards

SYRAH
Castelli & Pizarro Family Winery
Edwards Vineyard & Cellars
Mahogany Mountain Vineyard and Winery
Mermaid Valley Vineyard
Old Julian Vineyards & Winery
Pamo Valley Winery
Principe di Tricase Winery
Ramona Ranch Vineyard & Winery
Rancho San Martín Winery
Sky Valley Cellars
Sunrise Vineyards
Three Hills Winery
Turtle Rock Ridge
Vineyard Grant James

TEMPRANILLO
Barrel 1 Winery
Cactus Star Vineyard at Scaredy Cat Ranch
Castelli & Pizarro Family Winery
Rancho San Martín Winery

VIOGNIER
Barrel 1 Winery
Castelli & Pizarro Family Winery
Correcaminos Vineyard
Edwards Vineyard & Cellars
Mermaid Valley Vineyard
Old Julian Vineyards & Winery
Ramona Ranch Vineyard & Winery
Sunrise Vineyards
Vineyard Grant James

ZINFANDEL
Chuparosa Vineyards
Correcaminos Vineyard
Hatfield Creek Winery
Mahogany Mountain Vineyard and Winery
Mermaid Valley Vineyard
Principe di Tricase Winery
Three Hills Winery
Turtle Rock Ridge
Vineyard Grant James

Made in the USA
Monee, IL
12 November 2023